TESTED BEST

TESTED BEST

Edited by Jeffrey Feinman

FMC BOOKS

INTRODUCTION

My first realization of the potential of test kitchens recipes was a few years ago. I asked a gourmet cook for a few of her favorite recipes. I did not get original creations, family secrets nor famous cookbook treasures. Surprisingly she gave me recipes from company cookbooks, the back of labels or from corporate advertisements.

When I remarked that the source surprised me. She simply said, "Who do you think can afford to test, innovate, and research more than a food company? For example, think of my chocolate desserts. Who do you imagine would know more about chocolate than Hershey's and Nestle's?"

It made perfect sense.

There's a myth about American cooking and American taste--a myth that establishes hot dogs and hamburgers as the pinnacle of our nation's culinary excellence; that extols our fast food chains as the arbiters of the country's taste in foods. And it is a myth. There's a great tradition of fine American cooking dating from Colonial times.

Keeping America "cooking" is the giant recipe book industry. The industry was long characterized by the "super-chef". Cookbooks that became bestsellers required the name of a famous cook. In the past few years publishers have recognized that there exists a gold mine of recipes.

These were the recipes developed at America's Food Industry test kitchens. It should be no surprise that these recipes have great appeal. The obvious but (often overlooked) fact is that nobody can afford better to hire the finest cooks and home economists. They also have the budgets for the finest equipment and research library. And of course, no author, but a corporate author could afford the time and expense to test and re-test. Even a single recipe might be prepared dozens of times to assure quality of taste, texture, consistency and appearance.

Test kitchens can modify, improve and reformulate a single recipe as often as it takes to perfect it. After all many test kitchen recipes are "best sellers". That is, a recipe for inclusion on the back of a package, on a can or in a sponsor's advertising might be reproduced millions of times.

It's now your turn to enter the world of fine cooking . . . that comes out perfect (almost) every time! Each of the recipes in this book appear courtesy of the company indicated. You'll want to try many of them. Your family and friends will marvel at your new gourmet skills.

APPETIZERS

APPETIZERS

Appetizers are those tasty little morsels of hot or cold foods meant to whet the appetite when served with drinks before a meal or as a first course. But, with the cocktail party evolving as a major form of American entertaining, they may be the only food served on such an occasion. And, why not? Preparing appetizers has developed into a culinary art form of its own. Whether making and serving canapes, hors d'oeuvres, dips and dunks and spreads or relishes, cocktails or salads, shape, color and garnish is just as important as taste and texture. This gives creative cooks a wonderful opportunity to be fanciful and to have fun; to try new and exciting combinations of ingredients and to develop artistic presentations. It doesn't really make a difference what you call your appetizers but just for your own information here are a few definitions. The word *canape* translates from the French as "a couch", and the bread, cracker or pastry base is what distinguishes these small open face sandwiches from an hors d'oeuvre, also from the French. A literal translation of hors d'oeuvre is "outside the work" and, therefore, served before the meal.

Dips and dunks are more an American invention. Soft, mostly savory mixtures that can be made with little fuss they can be scooped up with crackers, vegetables or other nibbles. Spreads are firmer, meant to be spread on crackers or breads with a knife or spoon.

The following tested recipes are just a small assortment of appetizers of every kind that have become American favorites:

DEEP DISH PIZZA

1 loaf frozen bread dough*
1 1/4 cups Lawry's Extra Rich & Thick Spaghetti
    Sauce Mix, *prepared according to package*
    directions
1/2 teaspoon leaf oregano, crushed
12 ounces Mozzarella cheese, grated
6 ounces Provolone cheese, grated
2 ounces pepperoni, sliced
1 can (2 1/2 oz.) sliced ripe olives
1 cup sliced mushrooms
1 green bell pepper, sliced into rings

Optional additions and/or substitutions: sausage,
green chilies, anchovies, Canadian bacon

Let dough thaw and rise once; punch down and
roll out to fit a 15 1/2 x 11 - inch jelly roll pan. Spread
sauce over dough; sprinkle with crushed oregano.
Cover with grated cheese. Arrange the remaining
ingredients (and optional additions and/or substitutions) on cheese. Bake in 400⁰ F oven (on lowest shelf)
for 1/2 hour.

* Or your favorite pizza bread recipe.

Makes 24 pieces

Test Kitchen: Lawry's Foods, Inc.

BACON STUFFED MUSHROOMS

1 pound fresh mushrooms
2 tablespoons chopped onion
2 tablespoons butter
1 slice bread, torn into small pieces
1 cup (4 ounces) shredded Cheddar cheese
1 can (3 ounce) Oscar Mayer Real Bacon Bits

Remove stems from mushrooms and set aside caps; chop stems. Cook onions and chopped mushroom stems in butter until tender; add bacon bits and cheese. Mound filling in caps; place in shallow baking pan. Bake in 400°F oven 15 min. until cheese is melted. Serve warm.

Makes 15 to 20 pieces

Test Kitchen: Oscar Mayer®

WATER CHESTNUT CANAPES

1 package Frito-Lay[R] Brand Garlic and Onion
  Dip Mix
1 (3 ounce) package cream cheese, softened
1/4 cup milk
1/4 cup diced green pepper
1/4 cup diced pimento
1/4 cup chopped slivered almonds
1/2 cup diced cooked chicken or turkey breasts
1 (8 ounce) can whole water chestnuts

Drain chestnuts and slice. Combine Frito-Lay[R] Brand Garlic and Onion Dip Mix, cream cheese and milk. Add pepper, pimento, almonds, chicken or turkey. Mix well. Place mounds of mixture on top of each chestnut slice. Chill and serve cold.

Makes 30 appetizers

Test Kitchen: Frito-Lay ®

ALMOND CHEESE PINWHEELS

Pastry for double crust 9-inch pie
1 teaspoon Italian herb seasoning, crushed
2 tablespoons butter or margarine, softened
1 (3 ounce) package cream cheese, softened
1/2 teaspoon paprika
2 tablespoons freeze-dried chopped chives
1 1/2 cups grated Cheddar cheese
1 cup Blue Diamond[R] Whole Natural Almonds,
    chopped and toasted

Prepare pastry according to package directions or favorite recipe, adding Italian herb seasoning to dry mixture. Divide pastry in half. On lightly floured surface, roll each half into a 12 x 8-inch rectangle. Spread each rectangle with half the butter and half the cream cheese. Sprinkle each with half the paprika, chives, cheese and almonds. Press down lightly. Roll up tightly from wide end, seal edges. Slice 1/2 inch thick. Place on generously greased baking sheets. Bake at 450°F, 10 minutes, or until golden brown. Serve hot.

Makes 48 pieces

Kitchen: California Almond Growers Exchange

CORNED BEEF APPETIZER BALLS

1/2 can (12 ounce) Libby's Corned Beef
2 tablespoons prepared horseradish
2 tablespoons sour cream
2 tablespoons mayonnaise
3 tablespoons seasoned rye cracker crumbs
3 medium-size sweet gherkins, finely chopped
Finely chopped walnuts

Thoroughly combine all ingredients except walnuts. Shape into 16 balls; roll in walnuts. Cover and chill until serving time.

Makes 16 pieces

Test Kitchen: Libby ®

CREAM CHEESE SALAMI WEDGES

5 slices salami (approximately 4 inches in
   diameter)
1 (3 ounce) package cream cheese, softened
2 tablespoons milk
1 teaspoon lemon juice
1/2 teaspoon monosodium glutamate
1/2 teaspoon prepared mustard
1/4 teaspoon salt
1 teaspoon horseradish
2 tablespoons finely crushed Frito Brand
   Corn Chips

Blend cheese with`milk. Add remaining ingredi-
ents. Spread on slices of salami, placing one on top of
the other to form a stack. Chill. Slice in wedges.

Makes 12 wedges

Test Kitchen: Frito-Lay ®

ELEGANT CRAB MEAT BALLS

2 (6 to 7 ounces) cans crab meat
1 cup fresh bread crumbs
3 tablespoons Holland House Sherry Cooking
 Wine
1 tablespoon lemon juice
1 tablespoon grated onion
1 teaspoon dry mustard
1/2 teaspoon salt
Pepper to taste
Bacon slices (about 12), cut in halves

Drain and flake crab meat; combine with remaining ingredients except bacon; mix well. Shape into walnut-size balls. Wrap with bacon; secure with toothpicks. Broil under medium heat until bacon is crisp, about 10 minutes, turning to brown evenly. Garnish with parsley and lemon.

Makes about 24 servings

Test Kitchen: Holland House ®

HAM CORDON BLEU

1 (6 ounce) package Oscar Mayer Smoked Cooked
 Ham, squared
2 tablespoons bottled horseradish sauce
1 (6 ounce) package Oscar Mayer Sliced Turkey
 Breast Meat
8 slices natural Swiss cheese, each 4-inches square
1/4 cup butter, melted
1/2 cup crushed herb seasoned stuffing mix

Spread each slice of ham with horseradish sauce
and top with turkey slice and cheese. Roll and secure
with picks. Brush with melted butter and roll in
seasoned crumbs. Place on baking sheet and heat in
350°F oven for 12 minutes until cheese just begins to
melt*. Remove picks; cut into 1/2 inch slices. Serve
warm.

* Microwave in 12 x 7-inch glass baking dish
covered with plastic wrap (turning back corner to vent)
for 3 1/2 - 4 minutes.

Makes 64 pieces

Test Kitchen: Oscar Mayer ®

HIBACHI APPETIZER KABOBS

- 1 (5 ounce) package Oscar Mayer Brand Little Wieners
- 1 (5 1/2 ounce) package Oscar Mayer Brand Little Smokies Sausage
- 1 (8 ounce) can pineapple chunks, reserve liquid
- 1 lemon, sliced
- 2 oranges, cut into wedges
- 6-inch metal skewers

Thread skewers alternating Little Wieners, Little Smokies and fruits. Grill on hibachi. Brush with Honey Sauce*, turn occasionally until heated through.

Makes 8 servings

Test Kitchen: Oscar Mayer ®

Honey Sauce*

- 1/3 cup pineapple liquid (reserved from canned pineapple chunks)
- 1/4 cup honey
- 1 tablespoon lemon juice
- 2 teaspoons cornstarch
- 1/2 teaspoon celery seed
- 1/4 teaspoon paprika

Combine all ingredients in saucepan; heat to boiling, stirring constantly. Cook until thickened. Use to brush on kabobs. (Makes 1/2 cup)

MINI-QUICHES

1 can (8 ounce) refrigerated butterflake dinner
  rolls
1 package (8 ounce) Oscar Mayer Ham and Cheese
  Spread
2 eggs
2 green onions with tops, chopped

Separate dinner rolls into twelve pieces. Divide
each piece into three sections. Press dough sections in
1 3/4-inch diameter tart or muffin cups, stretching
dough slightly to form shell. Combine cheese spread,
eggs and onion; mix well. Divide mixture evenly
among shells. Bake in 375°F oven for 15 minutes or
until golden brown. Freeze extras; reheat on baking
sheet in 350°F oven for 15 minutes.

Makes 36 servings

Test Kitchen: Oscar Mayer ®

PORK SAUSAGE WON TONS

1 package (1 pound) Oscar Mayer Ground Pork
 Sausage
1 can (8 ounces) water chestnuts, drained, finely
 chopped
2 green onions, finely chopped
30 wonton skins, 3 1/2-inch square
Peanut or vegetable oil for frying

In skillet cook sausage over medium heat about
12 min., stirring and separating sausage as it cooks;
drain on absorbent paper. Combine sausage, water
chestnuts and onion. Place 1 tablespoon sausage mixture on center of wonton skin. Moisten corners of
wonton skin with water and fold up over sausage
mixture like an envelope. Pinch to seal. Heat at least 1-
inch oil in heavy skillet, wok or deep fat fryer to 375°F.
Fry wontons until golden brown, turning once. Drain
on absorbent paper. Makes 30.

Note: Wontons and skins should be covered with
moist towel when they are not being handled; they
have a tendency to dry out and become brittle.

Makes 30 pieces

Test Kitchen: Oscar Mayer ®

RUMAKI

2 pounds bacon
2 pounds chicken livers
1 (5 ounce) can water chestnuts
1 cup Holland House Whiskey Sour Mix
1/2 cup soy sauce

Marinate chicken livers and water chestnuts in the Holland House Whiskey Sour Mix and soy sauce for an hour. Fry bacon over low heat until just transparent. Drain. Cut bacon, chicken livers and chestnuts in half. Place one piece of liver and a slice of water chestnut on each half slice of bacon. Wrap and secure with toothpick. Cook under broiler until bacon is crisp.

Makes 6 servings

Test Kitchen: Holland House ®

SEAFOOD SPRING ROLLS

1 can (12 1/2 ounce) Bumble Bee Chunk Light
    Tuna*
1 cup vegetable oil
1/2 cup chopped green onion
1 carrot, shredded
1/2 cup slivered almonds
2 cups bean sprouts
1 tablespoon soy sauce
1/4 teaspoon pepper
1/4 teaspoon ground ginger
1 package (1 pound) egg roll skins
Water
Soy sauce for dipping

Drain tuna. Heat 1 tablespoon oil in skillet. Saute green onion, carrots, almonds and bean sprouts. Add soy sauce, pepper and ginger. Cook, stirring several minutes. Remove from heat and fold in tuna. Place two round tablespoons of mixture on the diagonal of each skin. Tuck flap pointing towards you in. Fold in sides. Roll up, seating with water. Heat remaining oil in shallow 7-inch skillet. Deep fry about 30 seconds on each side or until golden. Serve with soy sauce.

*or use 2 cans (6 1/2 ounce each) Bumble Bee Chunk Light Tuna.

Makes 26 servings

Test Kitchen: Castle & Cooke/Bumble Bee ®

SQUARE MEATBALLS

1 pound lean ground beef
1 egg
3/4 cup fine soft bread crumbs
2 tablespoons ketchup
2 tablespoons water
1/2 teaspoon Lawry's Seasoned Salt
1/2 teaspoon Lawry's Seasoned Pepper
1 teaspoon Lawry's Minced Onions with Green
   Onion Flakes

For Garnish:
Ripe olives, halved
Cocktail onions
Cheese wedges
Pickle slices

Mix together all ingredients except those used for garnish. Shape into a rectangle 8 x 6 x 1/2-inch on a jelly roll pan. Mark into 1-inch squares. Tope each square with your choice of garnish. Bake in a 400°F oven 15 minutes. Cut into squares and use a wooden pick to serve each square.

Makes 48 pieces

Test Kitchen: Lawry's Patio Kitchens

STEAMED CHICKEN A LA OLD BAY

3 pounds chicken wings, backs or necks
1/4 cup Old Bay Seasoning
1 tablespoon salt
1 cup water
1 cup vinegar

Cook pot should have a raised rack, minimum one inch high, add water and vinegar to just below the rack level. Layer chicken parts and sprinkle each layer with mixture of salt and Old Bay Seasoning. Cover and steam until chicken parts are done. About 30 minutes.

Note: To reheat: (especially for crisper hors d'oeuvres) Preheat oven to 350 degrees, place steamed chicken parts in oven, uncovered, on baking pan. Heat for 20 minutes and serve.

Test Kitchen: The Baltimore Spice Company ®

SUPER NACHOS

1 pound lean ground beef
1 large onion, chopped
1 teaspoon Lawry's Seasoned Salt
1/2 teaspoon ground cumin
2 cans (1 pound each) refried beans
1 package (1 1/4 ounce) Lawry's Taco Seasoning
    Mix
2 cups grated Monterey Jack cheese
1 can (4 ounce) chopped green chiles
1 cup grated Cheddar cheese
3/4 cup Lawry's Chunky Taco Sauce
Fried tortilla chips
Garnish with any or all of the following:
1 cup guacamole
1/2 cup dairy sour cream
1/4 cup shopped green onions
1 cup sliced ripe olives

Brown meat and onions; drain well and season with seasoned salt and cumin. Combine beans and taco seasoning mix; blend well. Add grated Monterey Jack cheese; mix together. Spread beans in a shallow, oval (10 x 15-inch) baking dish. Cover with browned meat and onions. Sprinkle chiles over meat; top with Cheddar cheese. Pour chunky taco sauce over cheese. (May be made ahead and refrigerated at this point--do not freeze.) Bake, uncovered, in a 400°F oven 20 to 25 minutes or until thoroughly heated. Tuck tortilla chips around edge of platter and garnish as desired.

Makes 10 to 12 servings
Test Kitchen: Lawry's

CREAMY TUNA DIP

1 (8 ounce) package cream cheese
3 tablespoons mayonnaise
5 tablespoons Holland House Sherry Cooking
    Wine
1 (7 ounce) can tuna
3 tablespoons chopped parsley
1 teaspoon steak sauce
1 garlic clove, crushed
1/2 medium onion, minced
Dash bottled hot pepper sauce
Salt, pepper to taste
Paprika

Mix all ingredients together, except paprika, in a large bowl.. Spoon into decorative crock, top with a sprinkling of paprika. Served chilled as a spread for small party rye bread or crackers.

Test Kitchen: Holland House ®

BEAN DIP NACHOS

1 (10 1/2 ounce) can Fritos[R] Brand Jalapeno Bean
    Dip
Doritos[R] Brand Tortilla Chips
Jalapeno peppers, sliced
Sharp Cheddar cheese, sliced or coarsely grated

Spread Doritos[R] Brand Tortilla Chips with Fritos[R]
Brand Jalapeno Bean Dip. Arrange on baking sheet.
On each chip place a slice or mound of grated cheese.
Top with slice of jalapeno pepper. Bake at 400°F until
cheese melts. Serve hot.

Test Kitchen: Frito-Lay [R]

CHEESY VEGETABLE DIP

1 package (3 ounce) cream cheese, softened to
    room temperature
1/4 cup (2 ounces) bleu cheese, softened
2 tablespoons frozen Minute Maid Lemonade
    Concentrate, thawed and undiluted
1 teaspoon horseradish
1 tablespoon chopped green onion
Assorted fresh vegetables (cherry tomatoes,
    zucchini, green onions, mushrooms, celery,
    carrots, etc.)

In small mixer bowl, combine all ingredients
except vegetables; beat until smooth and creamy. If
desired, chill until served. Serve with assortment of
fresh vegetables.

Makes 1 cup dip

Test Kitchen: Minute Maid ®

GUACAMOLE

1 avocado
1 teaspoon Holland House Liquid Daiquiri Mix
1 tablespoon mayonnaise
1 garlic clove, crushed
1/2 teaspoon freshly ground pepper
1/2 teaspoon salt
Dash bottled hot pepper sauce
1 small onion, minced

Skin and remove pit from avocado. Mash avocado and add remaining ingredients. Mix thoroughly. Use as dip for taco chips or spread on buttered party rye bread.

Makes 4 servings

Test Kitchen: Holland House ®

HORSERADISH DIP

1 can (15 1/2 ounce) Bumble Bee Pink Salmon
1 package (8 ounce) cream cheese, softened
1/4 cup dairy sour cream
1/4 cup horseradish
1/2 teaspoon salt
1/8 teaspoon garlic powder
Crisp romaine lettuce
Paprika
Crackers
Celery sticks

Drain salmon. Remove skin, if desired. Mash bones. Beat cream cheese, sour cream, horseradish, salt and garlic powder until smooth. Beat in salmon and bones until blended. Arrange romaine lettuce in a bowl. Spoon in salmon mixture. Sprinkle with paprika. Serve with crackers and celery sticks.

Makes 6 to 8 servings

Test Kitchen: Castle & Cooke/Bumble Bee ®

HOT CHILI-CHEESE DIP

1 (15 ounce) can Armour Star Chili - no beans
1 (4 ounce) can chopped green chiles
1 pound process American cheese, shredded
1 tablespoon Worcestershire sauce
Corn chips

Combine all ingredients, except chips; heat, stirring occasionally, over low heat until cheese melts. Serve as a dip with chips.

Microwave Instructions: Combine all ingredients, except chips, in a 1 1/2-quart glass casserole. Cook, covered, on high 6 minutes, stirring occasionally. Serve as a dip with chips.

Test Kitchen: Armour Star

SNAPPY BEAN DIP

1 (10 ounce) can tomatoes and green chilies
1 pound sharp American cheese, grated
1 (10 1/2 ounce) can Fritos[R] Brand Jalapeno Bean Dip

Heat tomatoes and chiles with the cheese until cheese is melted. Add Fritos[R] Brand Jalapeno Bean Dip and mix well. Serve hot with Fritos[R] Brand Corn Chips, Doritos[R] Brand Tortilla Chips; and Ruffles[R] Brand Potato Chips.

Test Kitchen: Frito-Lay ®

LIPTON CALIFORNIA DIP

In small bowl, blend 1 envelope Lipton^R Onion Soup Mix with 2 cups (16 ounces) sour cream; shill.

Try some of these delicious variations:

California Vegetable Dip

Add 1 cup each finely chopped green pepper and tomato and 2 teaspoons chili powder

California Blue Cheese Dip

Add 1/4 pound crumbled blue cheese and 1/4 cup finely chopped walnuts

California Seafood Dip

Add 1 cup finely chopped cooked shrimp, clams or crab meat, 1/4 cup chili sauce and 1 tablespoon horseradish

Makes about 2 cups dip

Test Kitchen: Lipton ®

THREE CHEESE DIP

2 (8 ounce) packages cream cheese
1 cup sharp cheddar cheese, grated
1/2 cup blue cheese, crumbled
1/2 cup Holland House Sherry Cooking Wine
1 tablespoon steak sauce
1 garlic clove, crushed
1/2 medium onion, minced
1/2 cup sour cream

Bring cheese to room temperature. Blend with electric mixer, gradually adding Sherry. Add remaining ingredients. Chill. Serve as dip with crackers or chips.

Test Kitchen: Holland House ®

BRANDIED CHEESEBALL

1 can (15 1/2 ounce) Bumble Bee Pink Salmon
1 package (8 ounce) cream cheese, softened
1/2 tablespoon brandy
1/2 teaspoon garlic salt
6 drops hot pepper sauce
1/2 cup diced pecans
Crackers
Celery sticks

Drain salmon. Remove skin, if desired. Mash bones. Beat cream cheese until light and fluffy. Beat in brandy, garlic salt and hot pepper sauce until blended. Beat in salmon and mashed bones until blended. Refrigerate until mixture is stiff enough to form into a ball. Roll in pecans. Refrigerate until ready to serve. Serve with crackers and celery sticks.

Makes 1 cheese ball

Test Kitchen: Castle & Cooke/Bumble Bee ®

CHIPPY CHEESE BALL

1 pound sharp Cheddar cheese, grated
1/4 pound Roquefort cheese, crumbled
1/2 pound cream cheese
2 tablespoons grated onion
2 teaspoons Worcestershire sauce
1/4 teaspoon cayenne pepper
1 1/4 cups crushed Lay's^R Brand Sour Cream
   & Onion Flavored Potato Chips

Have cheese at room temperature. Blend well with mixer or pastry blender. Add Worcestershire sauce, onion, pepper, and 1/4 cup of the crushed Lay's^R Brand Sour Cream & Onion Flavored Potato Chips. Shape into ball and roll in remaining Lay's^R Brand Sour Cream & Onion Flavored Potato Chips until completely covered. Chill well. (This cheese ball will freeze well.)

Makes 1 cheese ball

Test Kitchen: Frito-Lay $^®$

GOURMET CRAB RING

1 teaspoon unflavored gelatine
1/4 cup cold water
2 (8 ounce) packages cream cheese, softened
2 tablespoons dry sherry
3/4 teaspoon seasoned salt
1 (2 ounce) jar Dromedary Diced Pimientos,
    drained
1 (6 ounce) package frozen king crab meat, thawed,
    drained, cut up
1/8 teaspoon ground black pepper
4 tablespoons chopped parsley
Parsley springs
Crackers

Sprinkle gelatine over cold water to soften; then stir over hot water until dissolved. BEat into cream cheese until smooth. Stir in next five ingredients and 2 tablespoons of parsley. Pour into a 3-cup ring mold. Refrigerate at least 4 hours, or until set. To serve, dip mold quickly in warm water; loosen from the sides of mold with the tip of knife. Turn out on platter. Garnish base with remaining chopped parsley. Place parsley springs in center. Serve with Escort Crackers.

Makes about 3 cups spread

Test Kitchen: Nabisco ®

LIVERWURST SPREAD

3/4 pound liverwurst
4 tablespoons Holland House Sherry Cooking
  Wine
1/2 cup sour cream
1 small onion, minced
3/4 teaspoon fresh or prepared white horseradish

Mix ingredients in a large bowl until smooth. Use as spread for crackers, toast points.

Makes 6 to 8 servings

Test Kitchen: Holland House ®

SMOKY SALMON SPREAD

    1 can (7 3/4 ounce) Libby's Red Sockeye Salmon
    2 packages (8 ounce) cream cheese, softened
    2 tablespoons finely chopped onion
    1/2 teaspoon salt
    1/8 teaspoon liquid hickory smoke
    Cherry tomatoes, halved
    Onion, cut into rings
    Dill pickles, sliced
    Bagels, split, then quartered or wheat crackers

Drain salmon; reserving 2 tablespoons liquid; flake salmon. Thoroughly combine reserved liquid, cream cheese, onion, salt and liquid smoke; stir in salmon. Pack into lightly greased 3-cup bowl; chill several hours. With spatula, loosen spread from sides of bowl; unmold onto serving platter and surround with tomatoes, onion and pickles. To serve, generously spread salmon on bagels; top as desired, with tomato, onion or pickle.

NOTE: Salmon mixture may be packed into and served from ungreased bowl or crock.

Makes about 3 cups
Test Kitchen: Libby ®

WALNUT CHEESE LOG

1 pound finely grated Cheddar cheese
1 (8 ounce) package cream cheese
1/4 cup soft butter
1 teaspoon seasoned salt
1 1/2 cups chopped toasted Diamond Walnuts ®
2 tablespoons each chopped pimiento and ripe
    olives

Beat cheeses, butter and salt together until smooth. Stir in half the walnuts, all the pimiento and olives. Chill mixture for easy handling; shape into log or ball. Roll in remaining walnuts. Chill until firm. Serve with crackers. NOTE: If desired, 2 tablespoons sherry may be substituted for soft butter.

Makes about 1 1/2 pounds spread
Test Kitchen: Sun Diamond Growers of California/Diamond Walnut Kitchens

VEGETABLES

VEGETABLES

Once upon a time, in just the most recent past, America was the land of meat and potatoes. Vegetables were considered dull, something children should eat because they were "good for you," when all too often the "good" was cooked out. Artichokes, brussels sprouts, even broccoli were exotica. Leek, kohlrabi and fennel could only be found at ethnic markets.

Times and tables have changed. Americans are now eating lighter, healthier foods, less meat, fewer potatoes, lots more vegetables. Fresh, frozen, canned, in pr-mixed combinations, pre-cooked recipes, vegetables are among the most versatile of foods. You can steam them, bake them, fry them, braise them or broil them. You can serve vegetables buttered, spiced, crumbed, creamed or in a variety of sauces. Vegetables add color, taste, flair to meats, poultry and fish. And, vegetables alone can serve as a main dish.

Here are some of the best vegetable dishes in America:

BEANS & LENTILS

MOM'S BAKED BEANS

    1 tablespoon chopped onion
    1 tablespoon butter or margarine
    1 can (1 pound 5 ounce) Van Camp's^R Pork and
       Beans
    1/4 cup brown sugar
    2 tablespoons Stokely's Finest^R Tomato Catsup

    Saute onion in butter until tender. Combine onion with remaining ingredients in a greased 1 1/2-casserole. Bake, uncovered, at 350°F for 1 hour 15 minutes.

    Makes 4 servings
Test Kitchen: Stokely-Van Camp

CRUNCHY LENTIL BAKE

4 cups beef broth
1 bay leaf
1/2 teaspoon onion salt
1/2 teaspoon garlic salt
5 whole cloves
5 whole allspice
1 package (1 pound) lentils
1 package (12 ounce) pork sausage
2 tablespoons butter
3 cups sliced Dole Fresh Mushrooms
2/3 cup chopped green onion
1 can (8 ounce) tomato sauce
1/3 cup molasses

In a 3-quart saucepan, bring beef broth, bay leaf, onion salt, garlic salt, cloves and allspice to a boil. Add lentils; cover and simmer 30 minutes. Meanwhile, cut sausage into bite-size pieces. Brown well on all sides; cover and cook until no longer pink inside. Drain sausage on paper towel; discard grease. Melt butter in same skillet; saute mushrooms and onion until just tender. When lentils are done, remove bay leaf, whole cloves and allspice. Blend in tomato sauce and molasses. Add sausage, mushrooms and onion, tossing to mix. Turn into a 2 1/2-quart casserole dish; cover and bake in a 350°F oven for 30 minutes.

Makes 8 to 10 servings

Test Kitchen: Castle & Cooke/Dole ®

BEETS

ORANGE SAUCED BEETS

> 1 tablespoon sugar
> 2 teaspoons cornstarch
> 1 can (1 pound) sliced beets, drain and reserve
>   1/2 cup liquid
> 1/4 cup Minute Maid^R Orange Juice, reconsti-
>   tuted
> 1 tablespoon butter or margarine

In small saucepan, combine sugar and cornstarch; gradually add reserved 1/2 cup beet liquid and orange juice. Mix until smooth. Add butter. Cook over low heat, stirring constantly until thickened and clear. Add beet slices; heat through.

Makes 4 to 6 servings
Test Kitchen: Minute Maid ®

BROCCOLI

CITRUS SAUCED BROCCOLI

2 pounds broccoli
1/2 cup dairy sour cream
2 teaspoons frozen Minute Maid^R Orange Juice
    Concentrate, thawed and undiluted

Cut broccoli into serving size pieces. Cook in boiling salted water until tender, about 20 minutes; drain well. Season with salt and pepper. Combine sour cream and orange juice concentrate; serve over broccoli.

Makes 4 to 6 servings
Test Kitchen: Minute Maid ®

CARROTS

CARROTS VERONIQUE

8 medium carrots, cut into strips
1/4 cup frozen Minute Maid^R Orange Juice
    Concentrate, thawed and undiluted
1/4 cup butter or margarine
1/2 teaspoon salt
1/4 teaspoon cinnamon
1/8 teaspoon nutmeg
1 cup (8 ounce) seedless green grapes, drained, or
    fresh seedless grapes

Cook carrots in boiling salted water until tender, about 15 minutes; drain well. Add remaining ingredients; toss lightly. Heat for 3 to 4 minutes.

Makes 4 to 6 servings

Test Kitchen: Minute Maid ®

CARROT CASSEROLE

2 cans (1 pound) Stokely's Finest^R Sliced Carrots, well drained
1 can (10 3/4 ounce) cream of celery soup
1 cup grated American cheese
1/2 cup dry bread crumbs
2 tablespoons butter or margarine, melted

Combine carrots, soup and cheese in a 1 1/2-quart casserole. Mix bread crumbs and butter together; sprinkle over top of casserole. Bake at 350°F for 25 to 30 minutes.

Makes 8 servings

Test Kitchen: Stokely-Van Camp

CAULIFLOWER

GLAZED CAULIFLOWER

1 medium head cauliflower
1 tablespoon frozen Minute Maid^R Lemon
    Concentrate, thawed and undiluted
1/2 teaspoon sat
Dash pepper
1 teaspoon prepared mustard
1/2 cup shredded Cheddar or American cheese

Cook cauliflower in boiling, salted water until tender, about 20 minutes; drain well. Combine remaining ingredients except cheese; mix well. Spoon over cauliflower; sprinkle with cheese. Cover and let stand until cheese melts, 3 to 4 minutes.

Makes 4 servings

Test Kitchen: Minute Maid $^®$

CORN

CREAMY CORN 'N ZUCCHINI

1 medium zucchini, coin sliced
1/4 cup shopped onion
2 tablespoons butter or margarine
1 can (17 ounce) Green Giant Golden Cream Style
   Corn
2 tablespoons diced pimiento
1/4 teaspoon salt
Dash pepper

Saute zucchini and onion in butter until zucchini is tender. Stir in remaining ingredients and heat through.

Makes 3 servings

Test Kitchen: Green Giant ®

CHEESY CORN SCALLOP

1/4 cup butter or margarine
1/4 cup all-purpose flour
1 1/2 cups milk
1 cup shredded Cheddar cheese
1 can (12 ounce) vacuum packed golden whole
    kernel corn with sweet peppers, drained
1 can (8 1/2 ounce) Green Giant Golden Cream
    Style Corn
3 eggs, beaten
1 teaspoon prepared mustard
1 cup soft bread crumbs
1 teaspoon sugar
1/2 teaspoon salt
1/8 teaspoon pepper
1/2 cup cracker crumbs
1 tablespoon butter or margarine, melted

In large saucepan, melt 1/4 cup butter, add flour and stir until smooth. Gradually add milk and cheese. Heat over medium heat, stirring constantly, until sauce thickens. Add remaining ingredients, except cracker crumbs and 1 tablespoon butter. Spoon into a 2-quart greased casserole. Mix cracker crumbs with melted butter and sprinkle on corn mixture. Bake, uncovered in a preheated 350°F oven 1 hour or until center is firm.

Makes 6 servings

Test Kitchen: Green Giant ®

EGGPLANT

MEDITERRANEAN RATATOUILLE

1 can (9 1/4 ounce) Bumble Bee Chunk Light
   Tuna (or 2-6 1/2 ounce cans)
2 cloves garlic, pressed
1 eggplant, sliced in 1/2-inch julienne strips
1 green bell pepper, seeded & chopped
1 can (1 pound) whole tomatoes
1/2 teaspoon basil, crumbled
1/2 teaspoon salt
1/4 teaspoon pepper
1 bay leaf

Drain tuna. Heat about 1 tablespoon oil in pan.
Saute garlic until golden. Add eggplant and continue
sauteing adding oil as needed*. Add green pepper and
cook until just tender. Ad tomatoes, basil, salt, pepper
and bay leaf. Bring mixture to a boil. Reduce heat and
simmer about 10 minutes or until vegetables are tender. Remove from heat and fold in tuna. (Can be
served hot or cold.)

*Up to 1 cup of oil can be used

Makes 6 servings

Test Kitchen: Castle & Cooke/Bumble Bee ®

GREEN BEANS

GREEN BEAN BAKE

1 can Campbell's Cream of Mushroom Soup
1/2 cup milk
1 teaspoon soy sauce
Dash pepper
2 packages (9 ounce) frozen green beans, cooked
  and drained
1 can (3 1/2 ounce) French fried onions

In 1 1/2-quart casserole, stir soup, milk, soy and pepper until smooth; mix in green beans and 1/2 can onions. Bake at 350ºF for 25 minutes; stir. Top with remaining onions. Bake 5 minutes more.

Makes 3 to 4 servings

Test Kitchen: Campbell Soup Company ®

GREEN PEPPERS

SPANISH STUFFED PEPPERS

3 green peppers
1 pound ground beef
3 tablespoons chopped onion
1 can (15 ounce) Van Camp's^R Spanish Rice
2 tablespoons Stokely's Finest^R Tomato Catsup
Parmesan cheese

Cut green peppers in half lengthwise. team peppers with 1-inch water in pan for 5 minutes. Cool quickly. Meanwhile, brown ground beef and onion; drain excess fat. Stir in Spanish Rice and Catsup. Spoon ingredients into green pepper halves. Place peppers in baking pan. Bake at 350°F for 20 to 25 minutes. Sprinkle with Parmesan cheese.

Fills 6 pepper halves

Test Kitchen: Stokely-Van Camp

LIMA BEANS

THREE-BEAN BAKE

    1 (16 ounce) can green lima beans, drained
    1 (16 ounce) can navy beans, drained
    1 (16 ounce) can kidney beans, drained
    3 tablespoons vegetable oil
    2 medium onion, chopped
    3/4 cup catsup
    3 tablespoons vinegar
    2 tablespoons brown sugar
    2 teaspoons salt
    1 tablespoon prepared mustard
    1 cup crushed Lay's^R Brand Bar-b-q Flavor Potato
      Chips

Saute onion in oil until light brown. Add brown sugar, vinegar, catsup, salt and mustard, and mix well. Add beans and mix. Pour into 2-quart baking dish and top with Lay's^R Brand Bar-b-q Flavor Potato Chips. Bake at 325ºF for 1 hour.

Makes 8 servings

Test Kitchen: Frito-Lay®

MUSHROOMS

PEPPER-MUSHROOM SAUTE

2 tablespoons butter
2 cups sliced Dole Fresh Mushrooms
1/2 cup chopped green onion
1/2 cup julienne-cut green pepper
1/2 cup julienne-cut red pepper*
1 teaspoon dried Italian herbs, crumbled
1/4 cup dry white wine

Melt butter in a large skillet. Saute sliced mushrooms and green onion just until tender; remove from skillet. Add green and red pepper strips; saute lightly. Sprinkle Italian herbs over peppers; add wine. Cover and simmer 8 to 10 minutes until peppers ar tender. Add mushrooms and onion back to skillet. Heat thoroughly.

*Or 1/4 cup sliced pimiento.

Test Kitchen: Dole ®

VEGETABLE STIR-FRY

1 medium cucumber
2 medium onions
2 tablespoons oil
1 cup Dole Fresh Mushrooms, whole or halved
1 cup cherry tomatoes
Seasoning Mixture

Pare and slice cucumber 1/4-inch thick. Cut onions into wedges. Stir-fry onion in oil over moderately high heat 1 minute. Add remaining vegetables and continue to stir-fry 1 minute. Add Seasoning Mixture; stir lightly. Cover and simmer 3 minutes or until vegetables ar tender-crisp.

Seasoning Mixture:
1/3 cup dry white wine or water
1 tablespoon soy sauce
1 chicken bouillon cube, crumbled
1 teaspoon brown sugar
1 teaspoon vinegar
1 teaspoon cornstarch
1 clove garlic, pressed
1/8 teaspoon ginger

Combine all ingredients, blending well. Set aside.

Makes 4 servings

Test Kitchen: Castle & Cooke/Dole ®

PEAS

EASY HERBED PEAS

1 package (10 ounce) frozen peas
1/2 cup thinly sliced celery
2 tablespoons frozen Minute Maid^R Orange Juice
   Concentrate, thawed and undiluted
2 tablespoons butter or margarine
1/8 tablespoon ground marjoram

Cook peas in boiling salted water until tender, about 10 minutes; drain well. Add remaining ingredients; toss lightly. Heat through.

Makes 4 servings

Test Kitchen: Minute Maid ®

GREEN PEAS IN WINE SAUCE

2 (10 ounce packages) frozen small peas, or
    2 1/2 cups fresh young peas
1 1/2 cups thinly sliced celery
1 1/2 cups chicken stock or broth
3 teaspoons cornstarch
1 tablespoon water
1/3 cup Holland House White Cooking Wine
2 tablespoons butter or margarine
1/2 cup fresh mushrooms, sliced
Salt and pepper to taste

Combine peas, celery and broth in saucepan. Cover and cook gently until peas are almost tender, 5 to 10 minutes. Make a past of cornstarch and water. Blend with peas. Stir in wine, butter or margarine, mushrooms and salt and pepper. Continue cooking until liquid is clear and hot.

Makes 4 to 6 servings

Test Kitchen: Holland House ®

PEA PODS

CHILLED PEA PODS WITH WALNUTS

1 package (6 ounces) frozen La Choy Chinese Pea
  Pods
2 1/2 tablespoons sugar
1 1/2 tablespoons La Choy Soy Sauce
1 1/2 tablespoons white vinegar
1/3 cup coarsely chopped walnut

Cook pea pods in boiling water for 1 minute.
Rinse with cold water; drain well. Chill. Combine
sugar, soy sauce and vinegar, mixing until sugar is
dissolved. Add pea pods; toss lightly. Sprinkle with
walnuts.

Makes 4 servings

Test Kitchen: Beatrice Foods/La Choy®

POTATOES

SCALLOPED POTATOES

1 can Campbell's Cheddar Cheese, Cream of
Celery, Chicken or Mushroom Soup
1/2 cup milk
dash pepper
4 cups thinly sliced potatoes
1 small onion, thinly sliced
1 tablespoon butter or margarine
Dash paprika

Blend soup, milk and pepper. In buttered 1 1/2-quart casserole, arrange alternate layers of potatoes, onion and sauce. Dot top with butter; sprinkle with paprika. Cover; bake in a 375°F oven 1 hour. Uncover; bake 15 minutes more.

Note: Sliced cooked potatoes may be substituted for raw potatoes. Mince onion and reduce cooking time to about 30 minutes; bake uncovered.

Makes 3 to 4 servings

Test Kitchen: Campbell Soup Company ®

CRUNCHY TWICE BAKED POTATOES

4 medium baking potatoes, scrubbed and pierced
   with fork
1/3 to 1/2 cup milk
4 tablespoons grated Parmesan cheese
3 tablespoons butter or margarine
1/2 teaspoon basil, crushed
1/2 teaspoon salt
1/4 teaspoon marjoram, crushed
1/8 teaspoon pepper
Paprika
3/4 cup Blue Diamond^R Whole Natural Almonds,
   chopped and toasted

Bake potatoes at 400°F, 1 hour, or until tender. Cut
thin lengthwise slice from top of each potato; discard
slice. Scoop out inside of potato, leaving a thin shell.
Mash potatoes; beat in milk, 3 tablespoons Parmesan
cheese, butter, basil, salt, marjoram, pepper and dash
paprika. Stir in almonds. Pack potato mixture into
shells*. Place on greased baking pan. Sprinkle with
remaining 1 tablespoon Parmesan cheese and paprika.
Bake at 400°F, 20 minutes, or until browned.

*Note: Potatoes may be prepared ahead and
refrigerated at this point. Increase baking time to 25 to
30 minutes.

Makes 4 servings

**Test Kitchen: California Almond Growers Ex-
change**

SAUERKRAUT

APPLE KRAUT BAVARIAN

1 package (10 ounce) brown and serve sausage
1 can (1 pound) Stokely's Finest^R Applesauce
1 can (1 pound) Stokely's Finest^R Bavarian Style
   Sauerkraut

Brown sausage; stir in applesauce and sauerkraut.
Heat to serving temperature. Serve with mashed potatoes.

Makes 4 servings

Test Kitchen: Stokely-Van Camp

CANDIED AMARETTO SWEET POTATOES

- 1/4 cup butter or margarine
- 1/4 cup packed brown sugar
- 2 tablespoons Leroux Amaretto di Torino
- 1/4 teaspoon salt
- 3 cans (9 ounce) sweet potatoes, drained
- 9 large marshmallows

In a large skillet or electric fry pan* with SilverStone^R or Teflon^R, melt butter. Add sugar, Leroux Amaretto di Torino, and salt. Stir until sugar dissolves. Add sweet potatoes and marshmallows. Stir over low heat until marshmallows ar melted and potatoes are well glazed and heated through.

Makes 6 servings

Test Kitchen: Leroux ®

TOMATOES

TOMATO SOUR CREAM CASSEROLE

1 medium onion, chopped
2 tablespoons salad oil
1 (1 pound 12 ounce) can tomatoes
1 package Mexican style "sloppy joe" seasoning
   mix
1 (4 ounce) can green chilies, chopped
1 (5 1/2 ounce) package nacho cheese flavor
   Doritos^R Brand Tortilla Chips
3/4 pound Monterey Jack cheese, grated
1 cup sour cream
1/2 cup grated Cheddar cheese

Saute onion in oil; add tomatoes, seasoning mix and green chilies. Simmer, uncovered 10 to 15 minutes. In a greased, deep 2-quart baking dish, layer ingredients in order: sauce, crushed nacho cheese flavor Doritos^R Brand Tortilla Chips, Monterey Jack cheese, sauce, Monterey Jack cheese. Top with sour cream. Bake at 325°F for 30 minutes. Sprinkle with Cheddar cheese; bake 10 minutes longer.

Makes 8 servings

Test Kitchen: Frito-Lay ®

SQUASH

BAKED SQUASH MARSALA

2 small butternut or acorn squashes
1/2 cup brown sugar
1/4 cup Holland House Marsala Cooking Wine
1/2 cup butter or margarine
1/4 teaspoon cinnamon
Dash nutmeg

Cut squashes in half lengthwise. Remove seeds. Cook, covered in a small amount of boiling salted water in a large saucepan for 15 to 20 minutes, or until tender; drain. Scoop pulp from shells into large bowl, leaving a thin rim to hold shells in shape. Mash pulp with remaining ingredients. Pile lightly into shells; place in baking pan. Bake in 400°F oven for 20 minutes, or until heated through.

Makes 4 servings.

Test Kitchen: Holland House ®

SQUASH CASSEROLE

6 medium summer squash (yellow or white)
1 package Frito-Lay^R Brand Toasted Onion Dip
   Mix
1 1/2 cups boiling water
1/2 teaspoon salt
1/4 teaspoon pepper
3 tablespoons bacon drippings
1/2 cup grated American cheese
1/2 cup lightly crushed Ruffles Brand Potato
   Chips

Cut squash into medium slices. Place in boiling water to which the Frito-Lay^R Brand Toasted Onion Dip Mix and salt have been added. Cook until tender. Add pepper and bacon drippings. Pour into baking dish. Top with cheese and Ruffles Brand Potato Chips. Bake at 350^{0}F for 20 minutes.

Makes 6 to 8 servings

Test Kitchen: Frito-Lay ®

CHEESE AND GARLIC ZUCCHINI

4 medium zucchini
1 cup sliced Dole Fresh Mushrooms
1 tablespoon butter
1 tablespoon olive oil
2 tablespoons sliced green onion
1 tablespoon sliced pimiento
1/2 teaspoon garlic salt
1/4 teaspoon oregano
1 cup cheese & garlic flavored croutons
1/2 cup dry white wine
2 tablespoons grated Parmesan cheese

Cut zucchini in half lengthwise. Scoop out pulp with tip of a spoon, leaving shells about 1/8 inch think. Chop pulp. Saute mushrooms in butter and olive oil just until tender. Add zucchini pulp, green onion, pimiento, garlic salt and oregano. Cook and stir about 2 minutes. Whir croutons in blender to make crumbs. Add to vegetables along with 1/4 cup wine. Toss together well. Place zucchini shells in a buttered 13 x 9 inch baking dish. Fill with vegetable mixture. Slowly pour remaining wine over all. Cover and bake in 400°F oven 15 minutes. Uncover and continue baking about 10 minutes more, until zucchini is just tender. Sprinkle cheese on top to serve.
Makes 4 servings

Test Kitchen: Castle & Cooke/Dole ®

ZIPPY ZUCCHINI

    1 cup sliced onions
    3 tablespoons butter or margarine
    2 pounds zucchini, cut in thick slices
    1 can (16 ounce) tomatoes*
    1 envelope Good Seasons Italian Salad Dressing
        Mix

*Or use 1 medium tomato, cut in wedges.

Saute onion in butter until lightly browned. Add zucchini and tomatoes; stir in salad dressing mix. Bring to a boil; reduce heat, cover and simmer about 10 minutes or until zucchini is tender.

Makes 10 to 12 servings

Test Kitchen: General Foods/Good Seasons ®

ONIONS

GOLDEN GLAZED ONIONS

3 tablespoons frozen Minute Maid^R Orange Juice
    Concentrate, thawed and undiluted
2 tablespoons honey
1/2 teaspoon dry mustard
2 tablespoons butter or margarine
1 can (1 pound) whole onions, drained

In saucepan, combine all ingredients except onions. Cook over medium heat until bubbly, stirring occasionally. Add onions; stir to coat all sides. Heat through.

Makes 3 to 4 servings

Test Kitchen: Minute Maid $^®$

SALADS

ASIAN GARDEN SALAD

2 quarts torn spinach
1 cup bean sprouts
1 large orange, peeled and sectioned
1 can (8 ounce) water chestnuts
2 medium Dole Bananas, sliced
Honey Soy Dressing

Toss together spinach, bean sprouts and oranges. Drain water chestnuts and slice. Toss with spinach mixture. Just before serving, add bananas and toss with Honey Soy Dressing.

Honey Soy Dressing:
1/2 cup salad oil
3 tablespoons white wine vinegar
2 tablespoons honey
1 tablespoon soy sauce
2 teaspoons toasted sesame seeds
1/8 teaspoon garlic powder

Combine all ingredients in a screw-top jar. Shake well. Toss with salad. Makes 1 scant cup dressing.

Makes 4 to 6 servings

Test Kitchen: Castle & Cooke/Dole ®

CRUNCHY FRISCO SALAD

2 quarters bit-size pieces mixed salad greens
1 cup sliced fresh mushrooms
1 can (11 ounce) Durkee Mandarin Oranges
, drained and chilled
1 can (3 ounce) Durkee French Fried Onions
1/2 cup Italian salad dressing

Toss salad greens, mushrooms, and mandarin oranges. Just before serving, add French fried onions and dressing; toss gently. Serve immediately.

Makes 6 to 8 servings

Test Kitchen: Durkee

SOUTHWESTERN SALAD BOWL

1/2 head lettuce, shredded
1 pound ground beef
1/2 teaspoon salt
1 medium onion, chopped
1 (15 ounce) can kidney beans, drained
1 cup grated American cheese
2 medium tomatoes, cut in wedges
1/2 cup ripe olives
2 cups Doritos^R Brand Taco Flavor Tortilla Chips
Tomato sauce

Saute beef, salt and onion in skillet. Add drained beans; heat through. In a large salad bowl, layer in order: lettuce, Doritos^R Brand Taco Flavor Tortilla Chips, beef and bean mixture, cheese and tomato sauce. Repeat. Garnish with tomato wedges, ripe olives, cheese and whole Doritos^R Brand Taco Flavor Tortilla Chips.

Tomato Sauce:
1 (8 ounce) can tomato sauce
1/2 medium onion, chopped fine
1/2 medium tomato, cut into small pieces
1/4 teaspoon salt
1/2 teaspoon chili powder

Mix together and simmer for 10 minutes.

Makes 4 to 6 servings

Test Kitchen: Frito-Lay ®

GARDEN FRESH SALAD

2 envelopes Knox[R] Unflavored Gelatine
2 tablespoons sugar
1 1/2 cups boiling water
1 cup mayonnaise
1/4 cup Wish-Bone[R] Italian Dressing
3 tablespoons lemon juice
Vegetables

In large bowl, mix unflavored gelatine with sugar; add boiling water and stir until gelatine is completely dissolved. With wire whip or rotary beater, blend in mayonnaise, Italian dressing and lemon juice; chill, stirring occasionally, until mixture is consistency of unbeaten egg whites. Fold in suggested vegetables. Turn into 8-inch round or square baking pan; chill until firm. To serve, cut into wedges or squares.

Note: Vegetables - Use any combination of the following to equal 2 cups: chopped tomato, celery, radishes, mushrooms, asparagus or cucumbers.

Makes about 8 serving

Test Kitchen: The Lipton Kitchens/Knox [R]

GLITTERING GOLD SALAD

2 (3 ounce) packages lemon flavored gelatin
3/4 teaspoon salt
1 1/2 cups boiling water
2 cups cold water
2 tablespoons lemon juice
1 (12 ounce) can Green Giant vacuum packed
    Golden Whole Kernel Corn with Sweet
    Peppers, drained

Dissolve gelatin and salt in boiling water. Add cold water and lemon juice. Chill until thickened. Fold in corn. Pour into a 5-cup mold. Chill until firm. Unmold on a bed of leaf lettuce.

Makes 8 to 10 servings

Test Kitchen: Green Giant ®

GREEN BEAN CRUNCHIES

    1 (1 pound) can Stokelys Finest^R French Style
        Green Beans
    1 (3 ounce) package lemon gelatin
    1 envelope unflavored gelatin
    1/2 cup finely chopped onion
    1/2 cup celery
    1/2 cup coarsely chopped nuts

Drain beans, reserving liquid. Add enough water to bean liquid to make 2 cups. Bring liquid to a boil and add lemon gelatin, stirring until dissolved. Dissolve unflavored gelatin in 1/4 cup cold water and add to lemon gelatin mixture. Cool until slightly thickened. Fold in remaining ingredients. Pour in a 6-cup mold and chill until form. Unmold on crisp greens and serve with Tangy Dressing.

Tangy Dressing:
1/2 cup unpeeled cucumber, grated and drained
1 cup mayonnaise
1/2 cup finely chopped green pepper
2 teaspoons white vinegar
1/2 teaspoon salt
Dash pepper

Stir all ingredients together and chill before serving. Makes about 1 pint dressing.

Makes 8 servings

Test Kitchen: Stokely-Van Camp, Inc.

WALNUT JEWEL SALAD

1 (6 ounce) package strawberry flavored gelatin
1/2 teaspoon salt
2 cups hot water
1 (8 1/4 ounce) can crushed pineapple
2 tablespoons lemon juice
Cold water
1/2 cup chopped toasted Diamond^R Walnuts
1/2 cup diced celery
2/3 cup shopped raw cranberries

Dissolve gelatin and salt in hot water. Drain pineapple, saving syrup. Combine syrup and lemon juice with cold water to measure 1 2/3 cups liquid. Add to gelatin. Chill until mixture begins to thicken slightly. Fold in walnuts, celery, cranberries and drained pineapple. Turn into oiled 1 1/2-quart mold an chill firm, at least 4 hours.

Makes 8 to 10 servings

Test Kitchen: Diamond^R Walnut Kitchen/Sun Diamond Growers of California

RICE SALADS

BANANA RICE TOSS

    3 cups cooked drained rice
    2 ripe tomatoes, chopped
    1 green pepper, chopped
    1/2 cup cooked diced celery
    1/4 cup thinly sliced red onion
    3 Chiquita^R bananas, cut in 1-inch chunks
    French dressing

Marinate rice with 2 tablespoons French dressing and chill. Add remaining ingredients and mix together lightly with sufficient French dressing to moisten. Chill well. Serve in bowl on cups of crisp iceberg lettuce.

Makes 6 to 8 servings

Test Kitchen: United Brands Company/Chiquita ®

LIGHT SALAD MEALS

BACARDI CHICKEN SALAD SUPREME WITH FRUIT

2 cups cooked chicken or turkey
1/4 cup dark Bacardi Rum (80 proof)
1 cup celery, chopped
1 apple, peeled and chopped
1/2 teaspoon fresh lemon juice
1/2 cup raisins
1/2 cup canned pineapple tid-bits, drained well
1/2 teaspoon salt
1/2 teaspoon freshly ground pepper
1/2 cup lightly toasted almonds, or walnuts,
    chopped
1/2 to 3/4 cup mayonnaise

In a bowl, place chicken or turkey cut into 1-inch dice, or smaller pieces. Pour the rum over the meat and let marinate until you assemble all the ingredients. In a large bowl, add celery, chopped apple, and sprinkle the apple with the lemon juice. Add raisins, well-drained pineapple tid-bits, salt and pepper. Combine and add the chicken-rum mixture. Gently toss nuts on top, and add the mayonnaise, mixing carefully. Chill. Serve on lettuce leaves with a few grapes to garnish the platter.

Makes 6 to 8 servings

Test Kitchen: Bacardi

CHUTNEY HAM SALAD

1 can (1 pound 4 ounce) Dole Chunk Pineapple in
    Juice
2 cups diced ham
1 cup shredded Cheddar cheese
Crisp salad greens
1 cup dairy sour cream
3 tablespoons chutney

Drain pineapple reserving 2 tablespoons juice*.
Arrange pineapple, ham and cheese onto each of four
salad plates lined with crisp salad greens. For dressing,
combine sour cream, reserved juice and chutney. Spoon
over each salad to serve.

*Reserve remaining juice for beverage.

Makes 4 servings

Test Kitchen: Castle & Cooke/Dole ®

CRUNCHY CHICKEN SALAD

1/2 cup chopped, toasted peanuts
1/2 cup toasted sesame seed
2 generous cups cooked chicken, cubed
1/4 cup finely chopped onion
2 tablespoons soy sauce
2 tablespoons Holland House Red Cooking Wine
2/3 cup mayonnaise

To toast nuts and sesame seeds, spread in a shallow pan, place in 350°F oven for 8 to 10 minutes, stirring often. When cooled, combine with chicken and chopped onion. In a separate bowl, blend wine and mayonnaise. Pour over chicken mixture, tossing thoroughly. Serve chilled on lettuce leaves.

Makes 4 servings

Test Kitchen: Holland House ®

HAM AND HONEYDEW SALAD

3 tablespoons mayonnaise or salad dressing
3 tablespoons dairy sour cream
2 tablespoons frozen Minute Maid^R Limeade
    Concentrate, thawed and undiluted
1 teaspoon prepared mustard
1 pound (about 3 cups) cooked ham, cut into
    julienne strips
1 small cucumber, peeled and thinly sliced
1/4 cup thinly sliced green onions
1 honeydew melon, peeled and quartered

Combine mayonnaise, sour cream, limeade concentrate and mustard; mix well. In large mixing bowl, combine ham, cucumber and green onions, Pour mayonnaise mixture over; toss lightly. Serve ham mixture over melon quarters. If desired, serve on lettuce.

Makes 4 servings

Test Kitchen: Minute Maid ®

IRISH MAC SALAD

1 (12 ounce) can Armour Star Corned Beef,
    shredded
2 cups cooked elbow macaroni
1 cup dairy sour cream
1/4 cup chopped green pepper
1/4 cup chopped celery
2 tablespoons chopped onion
1 teaspoon salt
1 teaspoon prepared mustard
1/4 teaspoon pepper
Lettuce cups

Combine all ingredients except lettuce cups; chill
thoroughly. Serve in lettuce cups.

Makes 6 servings

Test Kitchen: Armour Star ®

LAYERED BUFFET SALAD

6 cups torn iceberg lettuce
1 cup chopped celery
1 (16 ounce) can diagonal-cut green beans, drained
4 hard cooked eggs, sliced
1 cup chopped green pepper
1/3 cup thinly sliced onion rings
1 (17 ounce) can Green Giant Small Early Peas, drained
2 cups real mayonnaise
1 cup coarsely grated Cheddar cheese

In a large salad bowl layer the lettuce, celery, green beans, eggs, green pepper, onion and peas in order given. Spread the mayonnaise over the top of the salad; sprinkle with grated cheese. Cover well and let stand for 8 hours or overnight.

Makes 8 to 10 servings

Test Kitchen: Green Giant ®

MACARONI CHICKEN SALAD

1 (7 ounce) package Creamettes^R Elbow Macaroni
   or Macaroni Shells, cooked and drained
3 cups cubed cooked chicken
8 ounces Borden^R Mild Cheddar Cheese, cubed
   (about 2 cups)
1 cup chopped celery
1/2 cup chopped green onion
1 1/4 cups Bama^R Mayonnaise or Salad Dressing
2 tablespoons chopped pimiento
4 teaspoons Wyler's^R Chicken-Flavor Instant
   Bouillon
1 teaspoon celery seed (optional)
Lettuce leaves

In large bowl, combine all ingredients except
lettuce; mix well. Chill thoroughly. Stir. Serve on lettuce. Refrigerate leftovers.

Makes 6 to 8 servings

Test Kitchen: Borden Kitchens ®

PATIO LUNCHEON SALAD

1 can (8 ounce) Dole Crushed Pineapple in Juice
1/4 cup white wine vinegar
3/4 teaspoon dry mustard
3/4 teaspoon salt
1/4 teaspoon tarragon, crumbled
1/4 teaspoon basil, crumbled
2 tablespoons vegetable oil
1/2 cup sliced Dole Fresh Mushrooms
4 cups Bud of California Salad Lettuce
1 cup alfalfa sprouts
1 medium tomato, cut in eighths
1/3 cup thinly sliced cucumber
1/4 cup thinly sliced red onion
1 cup cottage cheese

Combine undrained pineapple, vinegar, mustard, 1/2 teaspoon salt, herbs and oil; stir until blended. Add mushrooms and chill. Combine lettuce, sprouts, tomato, cucumber and onion in serving bowl. Sprinkle with remaining 1/4 teaspoon salt. Cover and chill. When ready to serve, toss with desired amount of dressing. Top each serving with cottage cheese.

Makes 2 generous servings

Test Kitchen: Castle & Cooke/Dole ®

SWISS SALAMI SALAD

1 (4 ounce) package Armour Star Hard Salami,
   sliced in thin strips
1 cup (4 ounces) shredded Swiss cheese
1/4 cup chopped green pepper
1/4 cup chopped celery
2 tablespoons chopped green onions
1/3 cup mayonnaise
1 cup croutons
Lettuce cups
Grated Parmesan cheese

Combine salami, Swiss cheese, green pepper, celery, onions and mayonnaise; chill. Just before serving, add croutons; toss lightly. Serve in lettuce cups; sprinkle with Parmesan cheese.

Makes 4 servings

Test Kitchen: Armour Star ®

VEGETABLE& SIDE SALADS
CELEBRATION POTATO SALAD

1/4 cup salad oil
3 tablespoons garlic flavored red wine vinegar
1 1/2 teaspoons salt
1/2 teaspoon dry mustard
1/2 teaspoon basil, crumbled
1/8 teaspoon white pepper
1/8 teaspoon dill weed
1 cup sliced Dole Fresh Mushrooms
1 1/2 pounds new potatoes
1/2 cup water
1 teaspoon chicken seasoned stock base
1/4 cup thinly sliced celery
1/4 cup chopped green onion
2 tablespoons sliced pimiento-stuffed green
olives

Shake oil, vinegar, 1/2 teaspoon salt, mustard, basil, pepper and dill wed together in covered jar. Pour over mushrooms and let stand while cooking potatoes. Pare potatoes and cut in large chunks. Cook in water with chicken stock base and remaining 1 teaspoon salt, just until tender, about 20 minutes. Drain well, and add to mushrooms and dressing while hot. Chill thoroughly. Add celery, onion and olives.

Makes 4 servings

Test Kitchen: Castle & Cooke/Dole ®

EPICUREAN POTATO SALAD

8 medium potatoes
1 medium onion, sliced
1 bay leaf
1 medium onion, chopped
1 cup chopped celery
1 1 /2 teaspoons salt
1 teaspoon celery salt
1 carton (8 ounces) Dannon Lowfat Plain Yogurt
1/2 cup mayonnaise
Hard cook eggs (optional)

Cover potatoes with water. Add onion slices and bay leaf. Cook, covered, until potatoes are tender. Remove potatoes from water; cool. Peel; cut into cubes. Combine with chopped onion, celery ad seasonings. Blend together yogurt and mayonnaise. Add to potato mixture, tossing lightly until well mixed. Top with hard cooked egg wedges if desired.

Makes 8 servings

Test Kitchen: Dannon ®

MIDDLE EASTERN YOGURT SALAD

2 medium tomatoes, sliced thin
1 medium cucumber, sliced wafer thin
1 cup plain yogurt
Salt to taste
2 tablespoons Holland House White Cooking
   Wine
1 teaspoon white wine vinegar
2 scallions, chopped

Rub cucumbers with salt; rinse and drain. Rinse and drain again after 10 minutes. Mix wine, vinegar and yogurt together in a large bowl. Add tomatoes and cucumbers. Toss lightly. Sprinkle with chopped onion. Chill.

Makes 2 to 4 servings

Test Kitchen: Holland House ®

OLD FASHIONED POTATO SALAD

1 cup Hellmanns or Best Foods Real Mayonnaise
1 cup minced onion
3 tablespoons white vinegar
2 teaspoons salt
1/4 teaspoon pepper
2 hard cooked eggs, chopped
3 pounds potatoes, cooked, peeled, cubed (about 6 cups)
2 cups sliced celery

In large bowl stir together real mayonnaise, onion, vinegar, salt, pepper, and eggs. Add potatoes an celery; toss to coat well. Cover; refrigerate at least 4 hours. If desired, sprinkle with paprika.

Makes about 8 cups

**Test Kitchen: CPC North America/Hellmann's ®
and Best Foods**

QUICK COLESLAW

4 cups (1/2 medium head shredded cabbage
1/2 medium cucumber, chopped
1/4 cup chopped onion
1/2 teaspoon celery seed
1/2 teaspoon salt
1 cup mayonnaise or salad dressing
1/4 cup frozen Minute Maid^R Orange Juice
Concentrate, thawed and undiluted

In large mixing bowl, combine cabbage, cucumber, onion, celery seed and salt; toss lightly. Combine mayonnaise and orange juice concentrate; pour over cabbage mixture. Toss lightly. Serve immediately.

Makes 4 to 6 servings

Test Kitchen: Minute Maid ®

SUNFLOWER SALAD

2 cups coarsely shredded carrots
1 cup thinly sliced celery
2 firm Dole Bananas, sliced
1/2 cup dry roasted sunflower seeds
1/4 cup oil
1 tablespoon frozen orange juice concentrate
1 tablespoon lemon juice
1/4 teaspoon salt
1/4 teaspoon pepper
Crisp lettuce cups

Combine carrots, celery, bananas and sunflower seeds. Stir together oil, orange juice concentrate, lemon juice, salt and pepper. Pour over salad mixture and toss lightly. Serve in crisp lettuce cups.

Makes 4 servings

Test Kitchen: Castle & Cooke/Dole ®

SLIM JANE SALAD

1 cup fresh bean sprouts
1 tablespoon lemon juice
1 tablespoon oil
1 teaspoon soy sauce
1 teaspoon sugar
1 medium Dole Banana, sliced
1/2 cup thinly sliced celery
1/2 cup thinly sliced pared cucumber
1/4 cup thinly sliced radishes
2 tablespoons sliced green onion

Crisp bean sprouts in ice water 5 minutes. Blend lemon juice, oil, soy sauce and sugar together. Mix with sliced banana. Drain bean sprouts well and toss with bananas. Toss in remaining ingredients and serve at once.

Makes 2 servings

Test Kitchen: Castle & Cooke/Dole ®

LATIN TUNA SALAD

1 can (12 1/2 ounce) Bumble Bee Chunk Light
  Tuna*
1/2 cup seeded chopped tomatoes
1/3 cup dairy sour cream
1/4 cup diced green chilies
1/4 cup diced celery
1/4 cup chopped green onion
1/2 teaspoon ground cumin
1/2 teaspoon garlic salt
Crisp salad greens
Tortilla chips

Drain tuna. Combine tomatoes, sour cream, chilies, celery, onion, cumin and garlic salt. Fold in tuna. Mound onto each of 4 salad plates lined with crisp salad greens. Serve with tortilla chips.

*or use 3 cans (6 1/2 ounce each) Bumble Bee Chunk Light Tuna

Makes 4 servings

Test Kitchen: Castle & Cooke/Bumble Bee ®

PACIFIC TUNA SALAD

1 can (12 1/2 ounce) Bumble Bee Chunk Light Tuna
3 tablespoons vegetable oil
2 tablespoons red wine vinegar
1 tablespoon toasted sesame seeds
1 teaspoon Dijon mustard
1 teaspoon sugar
1/2 teaspoon onion powder
1/2 teaspoon garlic powder
1/3 cup chopped green onion
1/3 cup diced celery
2 tomatoes
Crisp salad greens
1/4 cup mayonnaise

Drain tuna. Combine oil, vinegar, 2 teaspoons sesame seeds, mustard, sugar, onion and garlic powders until well blended. Stir in onion and celery. Fold in tuna. Slice tomatoes in half. Place on salad greens. Mound tomatoes with tuna mixture. Top each with a dollop of mayonnaise and sprinkle with remaining sesame seeds to serve.

*or use 2 cans (6 1/2 ounce each) Bumble Bee Chunk Light Tuna

Makes 4 servings

Test Kitchen: Castle & Cooke/Bumble Bee ®

SHRIMP ARTICHOKE SALAD

1 can (4 1/2 ounce) or 1 cup chopped cooked
    shrimp
1 can (6 ounce) marinated artichoke hearts,
    drain and reserve liquid
2 tablespoons frozen Minute Maid[R] Orange Juice
    Concentrate, thawed and undiluted
2 tablespoons tarragon vinegar
1/2 teaspoon salt
1/4 teaspoon sweet basil
1/2 teaspoon prepared mustard
1 medium sweet Bermuda onion, sliced
1 head lettuce, torn into bite-size pieces

Drain shrimp and thoroughly rinse in cold water;
set aside. Add reserved liquid from artichoke hearts,
orange juice concentrate, vinegar, salt, basil and mustard; mix well. In large bowl, combine shrimp, artichoke hearts, onion slices and lettuce; toss lightly. Add
vinegar mixture; toss lightly. Serve immediately.

Makes 4 servings

Test Kitchen: Minute Maid [R]

SHRIMP STUFFED AVOCADOS

1/3 cup mayonnaise or salad dressing
1/4 cup dairy sour cream
1 tablespoon frozen Minute Maid^R Lemonade
    Concentrate, thawed and undiluted
1 tablespoon chili sauce
1/2 teaspoon tarragon leaves
1/4 teaspoon salt
3 cups cooked, fresh or frozen shrimp
3 large avocados, halve, peel and remove pits

In medium mixing bowl, combine all ingredients except avocados; mix well. Top avocado halves with shrimp mixture. Serve immediately.

Makes 6 servings

Test Kitchen: Minute Maid ®

DRESSINGS

BASIC FRENCH DRESSING

1 cup Mazola Corn Oil
1/3 to 1/2 cup vinegar (lemon juice may be
    substituted for all or part of the vinegar,
    if desired)
1 to 3 tablespoons sugar
1 1/2 teaspoons salt
1/2 teaspoon paprika
1/2 teaspoon dry mustard
1 clove garlic

Measure into jar corn oil, vinegar, sugar, salt,
paprika, mustard and garlic. Cover tightly and shake
well. Chill several house, then remove garlic. Shake
thoroughly before serving. Makes 1 1/3 to 1 1/2 cups
dressing.

Zesty Dressing: Follow recipe for Basic French
Dressing, adding 2 tablespoons catchup, 1 tablespoon
lemon juice and 1 teaspoon Worcestershire sauce. Makes
1 1/3 to 1 1/2 cups dressing.

Mystery Dressing: Combine ingredients for Zesty
Dressing in small bowl. Add 1 unbeaten egg white.
Beat with rotary beater until thoroughly blended. Cover;
refrigerate. (Dressing thickens slightly on standing.)
Stir well before serving. Makes about 1 1/2 cups dress-
ing. Note: Dressing keeps well.

Spicy Dressing: Heat 1/3 to 1/2 cup vinegar. Add 1 tablespoon pickling spices (tied in cheesecloth, if desired). Let stand until vinegar is cool. Remove spices. Follow recipe for Basic French Dressing, using this vinegar. Makes 1 1/3 to 1 1//2 cups dressing.

Lemon Herb Dressing: Follow recipe for Basic French Dressing, using lemon juice for 3/4 of the vinegar, reducing range of sugar 1 to 2 tablespoons and substituting 1/2 teaspoon salad herbs for dry mustard. Makes 1 1/3 to 1 1/2 cups dressing.

Creamy Dressing: Follow recipe for Basic French Dressing, increasing sugar to 1/4 cup, omitting dry mustard and garlic, and adding 1/2 cup dairy sour cream and 1/4 cup catchup. Makes 2 cups dressing.

Vinaigrette Dressing: Follow recipe for Basic French Dressing, omitting paprika, dry mustard and garlic, and adding 1 hard cooked egg (chopped), 1 tablespoon chopped pimiento, 1 tablespoon chopped chives and 1 tablespoon chopped green pepper. Makes 1 2/3 cups dressing.

Diet French Dressing: Follow recipe for Basic French Dressing, decreasing vinegar to 1/4 cup, adding 2 tablespoons water and decreasing sugar and salt to 1 teaspoon each. Makes 1 1/3 to 1 1//2 cups dressing

Test Kitchen: CPC North America/Mazola®

CREAMY CURRY SALAD DRESSING

3/4 cup mayonnaise or salad dressing
1/4 cup Kikkoman Soy Sauce
2 tablespoons lemon juice
2 teaspoons sugar
1 clove garlic, minced
1/2 teaspoon curry powder
1/2 teaspoon ground ginger

Thoroughly blend together mayonnaise, soy sauce, lemon juice, sugar, garlic, curry powder and ginger. Let stand 1 hour before serving.

Makes about 1 cup dressing

Test Kitchen: Kikkoman International Inc. ®

CREAMY GARLIC DRESSING

1 cup mayonnaise
1 cup sour cream
2 garlic cloves, crushed
1 ounce Holland House White Cooking Wine
1/2 cup milk

Blend all ingredients, beating until creamy.

Makes about 2 cups dressing

Test Kitchen: Holland House ®

YOGURT MAYONNAISE

2 cups Dannon Plain Yogurt
2 tablespoons butter or margarine
4 tablespoons flour
1 cup milk
1 egg yolk
2 tablespoons lemon juice
1/2 teaspoon dry mustard
1/2 teaspoon salt

Melt the butter in a skillet and stir in flour. Add milk and stir over medium heat until thick. Remove from heat and beat in egg yolk, lemon juice, mustard and salt. Stir in yogurt slowly. Chill.

Makes about 2 cups
Test Kitchen: Dannon

YOGURT MUSTARD DRESSING

2 cups Dannon Plain Yogurt
2 tablespoons prepared mustard
2 tablespoons chopped capers
4 finely chopped scallions
2 teaspoons chopped dill
Salt & pepper to taste

In a bowl, blend all ingredients. Chill.
Makes about 2 cups

Test Kitchen: Dannon ®

ZESTY DRESSING

1 package Hidden Valley Ranch^R Dressing
1/2 cup mayonnaise
1 cup Dannon Plain Yogurt

Stir salad dressing mix and mayonnaise together.
Stir in yogurt. Chill

Makes 1 cup dressing

Test Kitchen: Dannon ®

POULTRY

POULTRY

Not too long ago in this country's culinary past serving a bird for dinner was reserved for holidays, special occasions...or Sundays.

Chicken every Sunday, became an indicator of well-being and affluence, so much a national tradition that it became part of our humor. And, in bad times it even entered politics as aspirants to public office promised a chicken in every pot.

As for turkey, it was saved for Thanksgiving feasts and, despite the fact that the earliest colonists found America abundant with fowl, many Americans lived without ever tasting duck or goose.

Today chicken is a menu mainstay. It's plentiful, economical, nutritious yet lower in calories than most meats. Poultry producers have branded their products and utilized TV to sell plump, fresh, ready-to-cook chickens available the way you prefer. You can buy chicken to roast, fry or broil; whole, in halves, quartered or in packages of the parts you prefer or need for a special recipe. Turkeys, Cornish hens, ducks are available in most supermarkets all year round.

Whether you want a dish that is easy, or an entree that is elegant, chicken is perfect. Here are a collection of recipes that contain a few new and surprising taste treats.

AMARETTO DI TORINO CREAM CHICKEN

1 (3 1/2 pound) chicken, cut up (or chicken parts)
Flour seasoned with salt and pepper
1 tablespoon butter
2 ounces Leroux Amaretto di Torino
1/2 cup chicken broth
1/2 cup heavy cream
4 tablespoons flaked, toasted almonds
2 tablespoons parsley

Roll chicken pieces in seasoned flour. In a skillet or electric fry pan* with SilverStone[R] or Teflon[R], melt butter. Add chicken and brown. Sprinkle with 1 ounce Leroux Amaretto di Torino. Add chicken broth. Cover and simmer 30 minutes, or until tender. Remove chicken to serving dish and keep warm. Add cream and almonds to sauce in pan. Mix over low heat. Stir in remaining Amaretto. Cook over low heat 5 minutes. To serve, pour hot sauce over chicken, garnish with parsley.

Makes 4 servings

Test Kitchen: Leroux

BAKED YOGURT CHICKEN

1 cut up frying chicken (2 1/2 to 3 pounds)
Salt, pepper
6 tablespoons butter or margarine
2 tablespoons flour
1 tablespoon paprika
2 cups Dannon Plain Yogurt
1/4 pound fresh mushrooms, cleaned and sliced
2 tablespoons fresh lemon juice
2 tablespoons chopped fresh dill or parsley

Wash chicken pieces and wipe dry. Add salt and pepper. Fry chicken in 4 tablespoons of butter until golden brown. Remove to buttered shallow baking dish. Sprinkle flour and paprika into pan juices and cook, stirring, for 2 minutes. Stir in yogurt and mix well. Spoon over chicken. Saute mushrooms in remaining 2 tablespoons of butter and lemon juice for 1 minute and spoon over pan. Sprinkle with the dill. Bake, covered, in preheated moderate oven (325°F) for about 1 1/4 hours, or until chicken is tender.

Makes 4 servings

Test Kitchen: Dannon ®

CHICKEN AND BROCCOLI CASSEROLE

1/4 cup butter or margarine
1/4 cup chopped onion
1/4 cup flour
1 teaspoon salt
1/2 teaspoon curry powder
Dash pepper
1 can (4 ounce) sliced mushrooms
1 tall can (13 fluid ounces) Pet^R Evaporated Milk
1 package (10 ounce) frozen broccoli spears,
    cooked and drained
1 chicken, cooked and cut in large cubes
1 cup (4 ounce) shredded Monterey Jack cheese

Melt butter in skillet. Saute onions until transparent. Remove from heat. Stir in flour, salt, curry powder and pepper. Drain mushrooms, reserving liquid. Add water to make 1/2 cup liquid. Gradually stir into flour mixture in skillet. Blend in evaporated milk until smooth. Add mushrooms. Cook and stir over medium heat until sauce begins to thicken. Arrange broccoli spears and chicken on bottom of a 13 x 9-inch baking dish. Pour sauce over. Top with cheese. Bake at 375°F for 20 minutes, or until bubbly around edges. Cool 15 minutes before serving.

Makes 6 servings

Test Kitchen: Pet Incorporated $^®$

CHICKEN BREASTS IN MARSALA CREAM SAUCE

   6 chicken breasts
   Juice from 1/2 lemon
   Salt, white pepper to taste
   6 tablespoons butter or margarine

Squeeze the lemon over the chicken, and sprinkle lightly with salt and pepper. Place in casserole. Top each breast with one tablespoon of butter, cut in small pats to cover all of each breast. Cook in 400°F oven for 15 to 20 minutes, or until chicken feels springy to the touch; do not overcook. Remove to serving dish; keep warm while making sauce.

Marsala Cream Sauce:
   1/4 cup beef stock or bouillon
   1/4 cup Holland House Marsala Cooking wine
   1 cup heavy cream
   1/2 teaspoon tarragon
   Salt, white pepper to taste
   Lemon juice
   Parsley

Pour stock or bouillon and the Marsala into the casserole with the remaining cooking butter and boil down rapidly until liquid is syrupy. Add cream, boiling until lightly thickened. Add tarragon, salt, pepper and lemon juice to taste. Pour sauce over chicken; sprinkle with parsley. Serve immediately.

   Makes 4 to 6 servings
Test Kitchen: Holland House ®

CHICKEN BREASTS PILAF

1 package (1 1/2 ounce) Durkee Roastin' Bag
    Onion Pot Roast Gravy Mix
4 cups instant rice, uncooked
1/2 cup slivered almonds
6 to 8 split chicken breasts, approximately
    3 pounds
1 to 2 teaspoons Durkee Curry Powder
4 1/2 cups water

Preheat oven to 350ºF. Place rice and almonds in oven cooking bag; top with chicken breasts, completely covering the rice. Combine gravy mix, curry, and water; pour over chicken and rice. Close open end of bag with twist-tie. Place in baking dish 1 1/2 to 2 inches deep and large enough to contain entire bag. Punch 4 small holes along top of bag. Place on rack in lower half of oven, leaving at lest 10 inches between rack positions to allow for expansion of bag. Roast in preheated 350ºF oven for 45 minutes. Cut top of bag; place chicken and rice in serving dish.

Makes 6 to 8 servings

Test Kitchen: Durkee

CHICKEN CONTINENTAL

1 can (8 ounce) Dole Sliced Pineapple in Juice
1 1/2 teaspoons flour
1/4 teaspoon basil, crumbled
1/4 teaspoon tarragon, crumbled
Paprika
1 whole chicken breast, halved and boned
1 tablespoon butter
2 thin slices cooked ham
2 slices Muenster cheese
1/4 cup dry white wine
1/2 teaspoon instant chicken bouillon
2 teaspoons capers
1/8 teaspoon cornstarch
2 tablespoons reserved pineapple juice

Drain pineapple, reserving juice. Combine flour, basil, tarragon and paprika and roll chicken breasts in mixture to coat lightly. Heat butter in skillet; arrange chicken, skin side down, and brown slowly over moderate heat for 10 minutes until well browned. Turn chicken and brown second side 10 minutes longer. Arrange 1 pineapple slice on each chicken breast. Top each breast with a slice of ham and cheese. Cook remaining pineapple in skillet with chicken. Cover and cook over low heat about 3 minutes until pineapple is heated and cheese melted. Remove chicken to serving platter. Add wine, bouillon and capers to skillet and boil rapidly. Stir cornstarch into reserved pineapple juice; add to skillet and continue cooking until mixture thickens. Pour over chicken.

Test Kitchen: Castle & Cooke/Dole ®

CHICKEN AND LOBSTER MARSALA

1 lobster (1 1/2 pound)
1/2 cup butter or margarine
1 chicken (2 1/2 pounds) cut in serving pieces
Freshly ground pepper to taste
1/2 cup chicken consomme or broth
1/2 cup Holland House Marsala Cooking Wine
1/2 pound fresh button mushrooms, or large
    mushrooms, sliced
2 tablespoons flour
2 tablespoons butter or margarine
1 cup heavy cream
2 tablespoons cognac

Place lobster in large pot of cold water and bring to a boil, cooking for 15 minutes. Let cool in liquid. Meanwhile, melt 1/2 cup butter or margarine in a large casserole and brown chicken on all sides. Add Marsala and mushrooms, and pepper to taste. Cover and simmer for 45 minutes. Transfer chicken and mushrooms to a side dish. In the casserole, gradually add roux made by blending flour with remaining butter or margarine; cook for about 3 minutes. Add cream and Cognac. Remove meat from chicken, cutting into cubes. Cut lobster meat into cubes. Add both, with the mushrooms, to the sauce. Heat thoroughly and serve.

Makes 4 to 6 servings

Test Kitchen: Holland House ®

COCONUT CASHEW CHICKEN RIBE

3 whole chicken breasts, split, boned and skinned
   (6 pieces in all)
1/3 cup CocoRibe Coconut Rum Liqueur
3/4 teaspoon ground coriander
1 large clove garlic, pressed
2 tablespoons cornstarch
1 1/2 teaspoons salt
1 pound fresh mushrooms, sliced
4 tablespoons butter or margarine, divided
1 cup heavy cream
1/4 cup chopped fresh parsley
2 tablespoons flaked coconut
1/2 cup salted cashews

Slice chicken breasts into strips about 1/2-inch wide and place in medium size bowl. Add the liqueur, coriander, garlic, cornstarch and salt; toss well; set aside 15 minutes. Saute mushrooms in 2 tablespoons butter 2 minutes or until browned; remove from pan. Add remaining 2 tablespoons butter to pan, add chicken breasts; saute quickly over high heat until pieces are lightly golden. Add mushrooms to pan; toss over high heat 30 seconds. Add cream; cook, stirring, until cream is thickened. Turn into serving dish. Sprinkle with parsley and coconut. Garnish with cashews. Serve over hot cooked rice, if desired.

Makes 4 to 6 servings

Test Kitchen: CocoRibe ®

CRUNCHY GOLDEN CHICKEN

2 1/2 to 3 pounds frying chicken, cut up
2 tablespoons milk
1 egg slightly beaten
2/3 cup cornflake crumbs
1 teaspoon salt
3/4 cup (6 ounce can) frozen Minute Maid[R]
   Orange Juice Concentrate, thawed and
   undiluted
1/2 cup honey
1/2 cup butter or margarine, melted
1/4 cup chopped walnuts or pecans, if desired

Combine milk and eggs. Combine cornflake crumbs and salt. Dip chicken into egg mixture, then roll into crumbs. Place on foil-lined baking sheet or pan. Bake at 350ºF for 30 minutes. Combine orange juice concentrate, honey, butter and walnuts. Pour over chicken. Continue baking for 25 to 30 minutes until tender.

Makes 4 to 6 servings

Test Kitchen: Minute Maid [R]

CRUNCHY CHICKEN CURRY

4 chicken breasts
1 fresh Dole Pineapple
1 cup sliced celery
1/2 cup sliced green onions
3 tablespoons butter
1 tablespoon curry powder
2 tablespoons flour
1 1/2 cups half and half
1 tablespoon chutney sauce or chopped chutney
4 strips bacon, cooked and crumbled
1/4 cup toasted sliced almonds
Hot fluffy rice

Wrap chicken breasts in aluminum foil and bake in a 400°F oven for 1 hour. Cool; remove skin and bones. Cut meat into large pieces. Cut pineapple in half lengthwise through the crown. Remove fruit, leaving shells intact. Core and dice fruit; then drain well in a strainer while making sauce. In a large skillet, saute celery and green onions in 1 tablespoon butter until barely tender. Remove vegetables from pan. Add remaining 2 tablespoons butter, then stir in curry. Cook about 1 minute. Stir flour into butter until smooth. Gradually add half and half, stirring smooth. Add chutney sauce and cook, stirring, until thickened. Fold in chicken pieces, pineapple chunks and bacon. Cook until heated through. Spoon into pineapple shells. Sprinkle with toasted almonds. Serve with hot fluffy rice.

Makes 4 servings
Test Kitchen: Castle & Cooke/Dole ®

GINGER PEAR CHICKEN TERIYAKI

3 tablespoons soy sauce
3 tablespoons light corn syrup
2 pounds chicken breasts, skinned, boned and cut into strips
2 tablespoons chopped crystallized ginger
1 tablespoon cornstarch
1 (16 ounce) can pear slices (or pineapple chunks)
1/4 cup Leroux Ginger Flavored Brandy

In a skillet or electric fry pan* or wok with SilverStone^R or Teflon^R, saute chicken strips in soy sauce and light corn syrup. Cook over medium heat for 5 minutes, stirring occasionally. Meanwhile, in a 2-quart saucepan with SilverStone^R or Teflon^R, combine crystallized ginger and cornstarch. Drain liquid from pear slices (or pineapple chunks) into saucepan; stir until blended. Over medium heat, heat pear liquid (or pineapple liquid) mixture to boiling. Add pear slices (or pineapple chunks) and Leroux Ginger Flavored Brandy. Boil 1 minute. Add to chicken mixture, stir and heat 2 minutes. Serve over rice.

Note: Thinly sliced beef can be substituted for chicken, if desired.

Makes 4 to 6 servings

Test Kitchen: Leroux ®

GOLDEN CURRIED BARBECUED CHICKEN

1 broiler-fryer (about 3 pounds) cut in quarters
1 cup warm water
4 teaspoons salt
1/4 cup Minute Maid^R 100% pure Lemon Juice
1/2 cup melted butter
1 1/2 teaspoons curry powder
1/4 teaspoon pepper

Place chicken pieces, skin side up, on greased grill and cook for 30 minutes over low heat, basting every five minutes with salt water. Blend remaining ingredients well and use to baste the chicken during an additional 30 minutes of cooking, turning and basting frequently.

Makes 4 servings

Test Kitchen: Minute Maid ®

GOLDEN OVEN-FIRED CHICKEN

2 (2 1/2 to 3 pound) broiler-fryers, cut up
2 eggs, slightly beaten
2 tablespoons milk
1 1/2 cups dry bread crumbs
2 teaspoons salt
1 teaspoon paprika
Dash of pepper
Squeeze Parkay Margarine

Dip chicken in combined eggs and milk; coat with combined crumbs and seasonings. Place in 15 1/2 x 10 1/2-inch jelly roll pan; pour margarine over chicken. Bake at 375°F 1 hour or until tender.

Makes 8 servings

Test Kitchen: Kraft ®

INDIAN CHICKEN CURRY

1/3 cup butter or margarine
1 large onion, chopped
1 cup chopped celery
2 tart apples, peeled and chopped
1 tablespoon curry powder
6 tablespoons flour
1 cup chicken broth
1/2 cup Coco Casa Cream of Coconut
2 cups (1 pint) half and half
3 cups diced cooked chicken, turkey or lamb
Salt and pepper

In a large saucepan, melt butter and saute onion, celery and apples for 5 minutes. Stir in curry and flour. Gradually stir in chicken broth, cream of coconut and half and half. Stir over moderate heat until sauce bubbles and thickens. Stir in chicken ad season to taste with salt and pepper. Serve spooned over rice.

Makes 6 to 8 servings

Test Kitchen: Holland House ®

LEMON BARBECUED CHICKEN

2 1/2 to 3 pound broiler-fryer, split in half
1 cup vegetable oil
3/4 cup lemon juice
1 tablespoon salt
2 teaspoons Durkee Paprika
2 teaspoons Durkee Onion Powder
2 teaspoons Durkee Sweet Basil, crushed
2 teaspoons Durkee Leaf Thyme, crushed
1/2 teaspoon Durkee Garlic Powder

Place chicken in a shallow pan. Combine remaining ingredients in a jar. Cover and shake well to blend. Pour over chicken and cover tightly. Marinate several hours or overnight in refrigerator, turning chicken occasionally. Barbecue chicken over hot coals for 15 to 20 minutes on each side, basting often with the marinade.

Makes 2 servings
Test Kitchen: Durkee

OVEN FRIED CHICKEN & BANANAS

2 chickens (about 3 pounds each) cut up
Salt and pepper
1 cup Coco Casa Cream of Coconut
2 tablespoons lemon juice
6 medium size bananas
2 1/2 cups cornflake crumbs
3/4 cup melted butter or margarine

Sprinkle chicken pieces on all sides with salt and pepper. In a bowl, mix cream of coconut and lemon juice. Peel bananas and cut each banana into halves crosswise. Brush chicken and bananas thickly with cream of coconut mixture and roll in crumbs, pressing firmly to make them adhere. Brush a baking pan with some of the butter. Place chicken pieces in a single layer into pan and drizzle with half of the butter. Bake in preheated 350°F oven for 45 minutes. Add bananas and drizzle with remaining butter. Bake for another 15 minutes.

Makes 6 serving

Test Kitchen: Holland House ®

SPANISH CHICKEN OLE

3 pound broiler-fryer chicken, cut up
2 tablespoons vegetable oil
2 stalks celery, chopped
1 medium onion, chopped
1 can (1 pound) tomatoes, cut up
1/3 cup Kikkoman Teriyaki Sauce
1/4 teaspoon pepper

Brown chicken on all sides in hot oil; remove from pan. Add celery and onion to same pan; saute until transparent. Arrange chicken, skin side down, on vegetables. Combine tomatoes, teriyaki sauce and pepper; pour over chicken. Cover and simmer 20 minutes. Turn chicken pieces over and simmer, covered, 20 minutes longer, or until chicken is tender.

Makes 4 to 6 servings

Test Kitchen: Kikkoman International Inc. ®

RANCH CHICKEN

1 (3 pound) chicken, about 4 cups
1 medium onion, peeled and left whole
1 rib celery
2 teaspoons salt
1 (10 1/2 ounce) can cream of chicken soup
2/3 cup tomatoes with chilies
4 cups Fritos^R Brand Corn Chips
2 cups grated American cheese
1 cup chopped onion
2 tablespoons shortening

In kettle cook chicken until tender with onion, celery, salt, and enough water to cover. Bone chicken and cube. Strain broth, reserving 1 1/3 cups. Saute onion in shortening. Add soup, tomatoes, and broth. Simmer 5 minutes. In electric skillet, spread a layer of chicken, Fritos^R Brand Corn Chips, sauce and cheese. Repeat, ending with cheese. Cover and cook at 250°F for 20 minutes. Lower temperature to 200°F and continue cooking for 40 minutes.

Makes 6 to 8 servings
Test Kitchen: Frito-Lay ®

RIPPLED CHICKEN SKEWERS

4 half breasts of chicken (about 1 1/4 pounds),
   boned and skinned
2 tablespoons soy sauce
2 tablespoons lemon juice
2 tablespoons white table wine
1/2 teaspoon dry mustard
1/2 teaspoon tarragon, crumbled
1/2 teaspoon salt
1/8 teaspoon crushed garlic
3 medium green-tipped Dole Bananas
12 cherry tomatoes

Pull out small inner filet from chicken breasts and cut outer portion in halves lengthwise, making a total of 12 pieces. Combine all remaining ingredients except bananas and tomatoes. Peel bananas and cut into quarters. Pour 2 tablespoons soy mixture over bananas to marinate. On each of 6 (10-inch) skewers, ripple two pieces of chicken, spreading chicken toward ends of skewers. Place on broiler pan. Broil 5 inches from heat 4 minutes each side, basting often with soy mixture. Remove skewers from broiler, push chicken pieces together and add 2 pieces of banana and 2 cherry tomatoes to each skewer. Broil 1 minute on each side, basting twice. Serve at once.

Makes 6 servings
Test Kitchen: Castle & Cooke/Dole ®

SARA'S COUNTRY CHICKEN

3 pounds chicken, cut in eighths
1/4 cup flour
1/4 cup olive oil
1 cup diced onion
1 garlic clove, crushed
1/2 pound fresh mushrooms, sliced
1 1/2 cups Holland House White Cooking Wine
1/2 cup pitted black olives
1/3 cup capers
1 pound can plum tomatoes, drained and cut up
1 teaspoon lemon juice
1/8 teaspoon each: pepper, basil, oregano, ground sage

Coat chicken parts with flour. Brown in olive oil. Remove chicken. Saute onion and garlic until golden. Add mushrooms. Cook 2 minutes. Add Holland House White Cooking Wine. Cook 10 minutes. Add remaining ingredients including chicken, cover, simmer 30 minutes

Makes 4 to 6 servings
Test Kitchen: Holland House ®

SENSATIONAL STIR-FRY CHICKEN

3 large half breasts of chicken (about 1 3/4 pounds)
1/2 cup vinegar
1/3 cup brown sugar, packed
2 tablespoons catsup
2 tablespoons soy sauce
1 chicken bouillon cube, crumbled
1 tablespoon cornstarch
1/2 teaspoon ginger
1 teaspoon salt
2 tablespoons oil
1 cup onion chunks
1 clove garlic, minced
3 medium firm ripe Dole Bananas, sliced
2 cups Chinese peas or 2 packages (6 ounce)
   frozen Chinese pea pods
1 cup sliced celery
1 cup sliced Dole Fresh Mushrooms
1 medium tomato, cut into wedges

Remove skin and bones from chicken and cut meat in bite-size pieces. Combine vinegar, sugar, catsup, soy sauce, bouillon cube, cornstarch and ginger, and set aside. Prepare all ingredients before starting to cook. Sprinkle chicken with salt. Heat oil in 10-inch skillet or wok, add chicken, onion and garlic, and cook 5 minutes, stirring frequently. Add bananas, peas, celery and mushrooms; stir-fry 2 minutes. Pour sauce mixture over and cook about 2 minutes longer, until glazed and thickened. Stir in tomato wedges and heat a few seconds.

Makes 4 to 6 servings

Test Kitchen: Castle & Cooke

SESAME CHICKEN AMARETTO

3/4 cup plus 2 tablespoons flour
3/4 teaspoon baking powder
1/4 teaspoon salt
1 1/2 tablespoons toasted sesame seeds
1 egg, lightly beaten
2/3 cup water
1 chicken (3 to 4 pounds), cut in pieces
Oil for frying
2 tablespoons butter or margarine
1 clove garlic, minced
1/2 cup chicken broth
1/2 cup Coconut Amaretto
3 tablespoons soy sauce
1 cup scallions, cut in 1-inch pieces

In medium bowl combine 3/4 cup flour, baking powder, salt and sesame seeds. Add egg and water; beat until smooth. Wash chicken, pat dry. In large skillet heat 1-inch oil. Dip each piece of chicken into batter; drop into hot oil (350°F on deep-frying thermometer). Fry several pieces at a time, about 20 minutes or until crisp and brown on the outside and cooked through. Repeat with remaining chicken. Meanwhile, in saucepan, melt butter, saute garlic until golden. Stir in remaining 2 tablespoons flour; cook over low heat 1 minute. Gradually add chicken broth, Coconut Amaretto and soy sauce; stir constantly until mixture boils and thickens. Add scallions; cook 1 minute longer. Serve sauce with fried chicken.

Makes 4 servings
Test Kitchen: Coconut Amaretto

SESAME SWEET N SOUR CHICKEN

        1 can (1 pound 4 ounce) Dole Chunk Pineapple in
            Juice
        1 (3 pound) frying chicken, cut up
        2 tablespoons butter
        1/4 cup apricot preserves
        1/4 cup catsup
        3 tablespoons soy sauce
        2 tablespoons red wine vinegar
        1 tablespoon oil
        1/4 teaspoon garlic salt
        1/4 teaspoon ground ginger
        2 teaspoons cornstarch
        1 large bell pepper, chunked
        1 cup halved cherry tomatoes
        1 teaspoon sesame seeds, toasted
        Watercress for garnish

Drain pineapple, reserving all juice. Saute chicken in butter until golden. Remove chicken. Melt apricot preserves in skillet with pan drippings. Stir in 1/2 cup reserved pineapple juice, catsup, soy sauce, vinegar, oil, garlic salt and ground ginger. Return chicken to skillet. Cover and simmer 25 minutes, until tender. Remove chicken to warmed serving platter. Combine cornstarch with remaining pineapple juice; pour into pan juices. Cook, stirring constantly, until sauce boils and thickens. Add pineapple chunks, pepper and tomatoes, cooking until pepper is tender-crisp. Spoon over chicken. Sprinkle with sesame seeds and garnish with watercress to serve.

        Makes 6 servings
Test Kitchen: Castle & Cooke/Dole ®

STIR-FRY CHICKEN

Stir-frying is fast. Make sure all your ingredients are ready to toss in the pan when the oil is hot!

1 can (8 ounce) Dole Chunk Pineapple in Juice
3 chicken thighs
1 tablespoon cornstarch
3 tablespoons vegetable oil
1 cup quartered Dole Fresh Mushrooms
2 tablespoons soy sauce
1/4 teaspoon garlic powder
1/8 teaspoon ginger powder
1 small tomato, seeded & chopped
2 green onions, sliced
Hot fluffy rice

Drain pineapple*. Skin and bone chicken; cut into 1-inch pieces. Dredge chicken with cornstarch. Heat oil in large heavy skillet or wok. Add chicken and stir-fry on high heat 2 minutes. Add mushrooms and soy sauce. Sprinkle with garlic and ginger. Reduce heat and simmer uncovered 3 to 5 minutes, stirring constantly. Stir in tomato and pineapple. Cook 1 minute longer. Top with sliced green onions. Serve over hot fluffy rice.

*Reserve juice for beverage.

Makes 2 servings
Test Kitchen: Castle & Cooke/Dole ®

GLORIFIED CHICKEN

2 pounds chicken parts
2 tablespoons shortening
1 can Campbells Cheddar Cheese, Cream of Celery, Chicken or Mushroom Soup

In skillet, brown chicken in shortening. Pour off fat. Stir in soup. Cover: cook over low heat 45 minutes or until tender. Stir occasionally.

Makes 4 servings
Test Kitchen: Campbell Soup Company ®

ZESTY CORN-CRISPED CHICKEN

1 egg
1/4 cup Kikkoman Soy Sauce
3 pound broiler-fryer chicken, cut up
1 1/2 cups corn flake crumbs

Beat egg in shallow dish or pan; stir in soy sauce until well blended. Dip chicken pieces into egg mixture, then coat with corn flake crumbs. Place in single layer in foil-lined or well-greased shallow baking pan; do not crowd. Bake in 350ºF oven about 1 hour, or until chicken is tender. Serve with additional soy sauce, if desired.

Makes 6 servings
Test Kitchen: Kikkoman International Inc. ®

CORNISH HENS

ROAST STUFFED CORNISH HENS COCO CASA

2 Rock Cornish Hens
Salt
Pepper
Thyme
1 clove garlic, crushed
1 cup mixed dried fruit
1 cup seasoned croutons
1/2 stick unsalted butter, melted
1/4 cup Coco Casa Cream of Coconut
1/2 cup frozen orange concentrate, undiluted
1/2 cup Coco Casa Cream of Coconut
2 tablespoons Holland House Sherry Cooking
   Wine

Wash and dry hens. Rub lightly with salt, pepper, thyme and garlic. Stuff and skewer. Brush with basting sauce and roast in pre-heated 400°F oven, basting every ten minutes. Roast hens for 1 to 1 1/2 hours, or until tender when pierced with a fork. Spoon pan juices over hens before serving.

Stuffing: Cut fruit in small chunks and toss with croutons, butter and 1/4 cup cream of coconut.
Basting sauce: Mix together orange concentrate, 1/2 cup cream of coconut and sherry.

Makes 4 servings

Test Kitchen: Holland House ®

DUCK

BACARDI PLUM DUCK WITH PLUM RUM SAUCE

2 (5 pound) ducks, thawed
Salt
Pepper
Ginger
1/2 cup dark Bacardi Rum (80 proof)

Season inside and outside of ducks with salt, pepper and ginger. Place in a roasting plan, backs up in a pre-heated 325°F oven. Roast 1 hour, drain off fat, turn ducks breasts up and continue to roast 1 1/2 more hours, drain fat every 1/2 hour. Baste with rum every 15 minutes the last 45 minutes. When roast is done spoon over each duck 1/4 cup of plum rum sauce, allow to stay in oven for 10 minutes longer, then serve with more sauce on the side

LUSCIOUS PLUM RUM SAUCE

2 tablespoons butter
2 tablespoons cornstarch
1 1/2 cups water
3 tablespoons brown sugar
1/4 teaspoon ground ginger
4 or 5 red or purple plums, sliced
1/4 cup dark Bacardi Rum (80 proof)

In a pan blend butter and cornstarch, stir over lowheat. Gradually add water, sugar and ginger. Stir and cook 3 or 4 minutes. Add plums, stir and cook until plums are soft. Add rum, blend and remove from heat. Serve warm over ducks or on the side. May be reheated if sauce cools.

Makes 6 to 8 servings

Test Kitchen: Bacardi

TURKEY

ORANGE SHERRY TURKEY

8 to 12 pounds turkey
3 cups water
1 teaspoon salt
1 teaspoon rosemary
3 cubes bouillon or 3 teaspoons instant chicken
   bouillon
6 slices bacon
1/2 cup sliced green onion
2 tablespoons butter or margerine
1 can (8 ounce) water chestnuts, drain and slice
3/4 cup (6 ounce) can frozen Minute Maid Orange Juice Concentrate, thawed and undiluted
1/4 cup sherry

Thaw turkey and prepare for baking as directed on package. In medium saucepan, combine water, salt; rosemary and bouillon. Bring to a boil; add uncooked brown rice. Cover and simmer for 30 minutes until all liquid has been absorbed. Meanwhile, fry bacon until crisp; drain and crumble. Add bacon pieces, green onion, butter and water chestnuts to rice; mix well. Add 3 tablespoons orange juice concentrate; reserve remainder of can for basting. Stuff cavity and neck portion of turkey with rice mixture. Place in roasting pan or 13 x 9-inch baking pan. Place pan and turkey in

Bake at 325F for 4 to 4 1/2 hours until tender. Remove paper bag. Combine remaining orange juice concentrate and sherry; mix well. Brush on turkey. Continue to bake for 15 to 20 minutes, basting frequently, until golden brown.

Makes 10 to 12 servings

Test Kitchen: Minute Maid ®

ZUCCHINI-TURKEY BAKE

4 zucchini, cut in 1/2 inch slices
3/4 cup sliced carrots
Water
1/4 teaspoon salt
1/2 cup chopped onion
6 tablespoons butter or margarine
2 1/4 cups seasoned stuffing cubes
2 cups cubed cooked Armour Golden Star Young Turkey
1 (10 3/4 ounce) can cream of chicken soup
1 cup dairy sour cream
1/2 cup grated Parmesan cheese

Heat oven to 350°F. In covered saucepan, simmer zucchini and carrots in salted water to cover 15 minutes; drain. In large fry pan, cook onion in 1/4 cup butter or margarine 10 minutes. Stir in 1 1/2 cups stuffing cubes, turkey, soup and sour cream; gently fold in cooked vegetables. Pour mixture into greased 2-quart casserole. Top with remaining stuffing cubes and Parmesan cheese. Bake at 350°F 35 to 40 minutes.

Makes 6 to 8 servings
Test Kitchen: Armour Star ®

TURKEY PAPRIKASH

1 envelope (7/8 ounce) French's Onion Gravy
    Mix
1 cup water
1 tablespoon catchup
1/2 teaspoon paprika
2 cups diced cooked turkey
1/2 cup dairy sour cream
1/4 cup chopped or sliced pimiento
Cooked egg noodles

Combine contents of gravy mix envelope, water, catchup, paprika, and turkey. Heat to boiling, stirring occasionally. Simmer 5 minutes. Stir in sour cream and pimiento. Serve over cooked noodles.

Makes 4 to 5 servings

Test Kitchen: The R. T. French Company ®

ROAST TURKEY WITH GRANOLA STUFFING

- 1 teaspoon Armour Star Chicken Flavor Instant Bouillon or 1 Armour Star Chicken Flavor Bouillon Cube dissolved in 1 cup boiling water
- 4 cups granola cereal
- 4 cups dry whole wheat bread cubes
- 3 cups coarsely chopped cranberries
- 1 cup chopped onion
- 4 eggs, beaten
- 1/2 cup chopped parsley
- 3 tablespoons grated lemon rind
- 2 teaspoons salt
- 1/2 teaspoon pepper
- 1 (12 to 14 pound) Armour Golden Star Young Turkey, thawed

Heat oven to 325°F. Combine all ingredients except turkey; toss lightly. Makes 12 cups stuffing. Loosely stuff neck and body cavities of turkey; roast according to label instructions. Place extra stuffing in greased 2-quart casserole. Bake, covered, at 325°F 30 to 35 minutes.

Test Kitchen: Armour Star ®

ROAST TURKEY WITH APPLE-YAM DRESSING

1 (3 to 8 pound) Armour Golden Star Boneless
    Young Turkey, thawed
2 cups chopped apples
2/3 cup chopped onion
3/4 cup butter or margarine
2 (16 ounce) cans yams, drained, mashed
2 tablespoons sugar
2 teaspoons salt
1/2 teaspoon nutmeg
1/2 teaspoon cinnamon
4 cups soft bread cubes

Heat oven to 350°F. Roast turkey according to label instructions. While turkey is roasting, in fry pan, cook apples and onion in butter or margarine 10 minutes; combine with remaining ingredients. Toss lightly; set aside. One hour before turkey is scheduled to be done, remove turkey from oven. Lift turkey and rack from pan. Scrape drippings from pan to use for gravy. Return turkey to pan with out rack; turn turkey over. Brush turkey with some of reserved pan drippings. Spoon dressing into pan around turkey. Return turkey and dressing to 350°F oven; continue roasting until done.

Test Kitchen: Armour Star ®

SEAFOOD

SEAFOOD

The seas and inland waters of the world provide us with a remarkable bounty of edible food in such variety and abundance that fish is a major part of the diet of most of the world's population.

In Italy where they call their harvest from the Adriatic and Mediterranean frutti di mare, fruit of the sea, fish is as important as pasta to the national cuisine. The Japanese frequent sushi bars to savor the delicacy of precisely cut and delicately served raw fish. And, in Mexico and other Latin American countries, seviche, thinly sliced fish marinated in lime, is a refreshing dish favored in warm weather.

Yet, in the United States where crab feasts, fish fries, oyster roasts and clam and lobster bakes are part of our culinary heritage; where the seafood of New England, Maryland, Louisiana and San Francisco is renown, fish is not considered popular.

Remarkable when one remembers that the earliest colonists depended on fish for their survival; that subsequent settlers delighted in the variety of seafood, feasting on shrimp, crab and other fish; that in the mid-nineteenth century ingenious ways were found to pack oysters and send them express to our landlocked states and throughout the populated parts of America they were as popular as pizza is now.

But, in this era of lighter diets and more sophisticated tastes, fish is finding its way back to the American table. Fresh, frozen, smoked or canned, it is available all year round. Serve it hot or cold, marinated or raw. There is no end to the ways it can be prepared—sauted, broiled, pan-fried, braised, baked, poached or steamed. Serve it plain, or in a sauce or mixed with other foods.

Choose from a wondrous variety. These are the salt water fish: bass, bluefish, cod, flounder, haddock, halibut, herring, mackerel, pompano, salmon, shad, sole, sturgeon, swordfish and tuna; fresh water fish: carp, catfish, pike, perch, smelt, trout and white fish; shellfish: abalone, clams, crabs, crayfish, lobsters, mussels, oysters, scallops and shrimp. And, there are more to discover.

Here are some of the tested fish recipes that can change your dining habits.

CHINESE FISH WITH PISTACHIOS

1 pound lean firm-fleshed white fish fillets (cod, flounder, sole, haddock, halibut)
Ground Pepper and lemon juice or salt
1/4 cup shelled natural California pistachios
1 tablespoon vegetable oil
1 cup sliced celery
1 cup thin onion wedges
1 minced garlic
1 tablespoon grated fresh ginger root
1 cup tomato cubes
4 servings (1/2 cup each) hot cooked rice

Season both sides of fish fillets with pepper and lemon juice (or salt). Roll up fillets and place seam down on heatprooof plate. Saute pistachios in oil in large skillet; remove from pan with slotted spoon, leaving oil. Add celery, onion, garlic and ginger to skillet; saute until nearly tender. Add tomato and cook, stirring until hot. Turn vegetables onto platter and keep warm. Place plate of fish on rack over 1/2-inch boiling water in the skillet. Cover and steam 7 to 9 minutes or until fish flakes with fork. Transfer fish to the top of vegetables. Sprinkle with roasted pistachios. Serve with hot rice.

Makes 4 servings

Test Kitchen: California Pistachio Commission

CRAB CAKES & SEAFOOD CAKES

2 slices bread, crusts removed
1 pound shrimp or flaked cooked fish
1 egg, beaten
1 to 3 teaspoons Old Bay Seasoning (depending
   on heat preference)
1 tablespoon baking powder
1 tablespoon chopped parsley
1 tablespoon Worcestershire sauce
1 tablespoon mayonnaise or salad dressing

Crumble bread slices and combine with remaining ingredients. Shape into patties. Fry quickly in 3 to 4 tablespoons hot oil until brown.

Note: Crab meat, tuna or salmon may be used also.

Makes 6 to 8 cakes

Test Kitchen: The Baltimore Spice Company ®

CRABMEAT FLORENTINE

1 package (6 ounce) fresh or frozen crabmeat
1 package (10 ounces) frozen chopped spinach
1 cup sliced Dole Fresh Mushrooms
2 tablespoons butter
2 tablespoons flour
1 teaspoon garlic salt
1/4 teaspoon freshly ground black pepper
1/4 cup dry sherry
1/2 cup milk
1 cup dairy sour cream
1 cup grated Swiss cheese

Thaw crabmeat in refrigerator overnight. Thaw and drain spinach. Saute mushrooms in butter in a large skillet until golden. Blend in flour, garlic salt, pepper, sherry and milk. Stir in sour cream, spinach and crabmeat with all liquid. Cook, stirring constantly until mixture boils and thickens. Spoon into 4 large baking shells or individual ramekins. Sprinkle with cheese. Place under broiler about 5 inches from heat until cheese is bubbly and browned. Serve at once.

Makes 4 servings

Test Kitchen: Castle & Cooke/Dole ®

CRAB STEW

1 1/2 pounds crabmeat, fresh or canned
1 tablespoon butter or margarine
Salt and white pepper to taste
1 pint milk
1 pint heavy cream
Several dashes bottled hot pepper sauce
1 teaspoon Worcestershire sauce
3/4 cup Holland House Marsala Cooking Wine
1 tablespoon parsley

In a soup pot, simmer crab, butter or margarine, salt and pepper and milt for 10 minutes. Add cream and hot seasonings, and bring just to boiling point, stirring as little as possible. Remove from heat and add Marsala. Serve in soup bowls or cups with a sprinkling of parsley.

Makes 6 servings
Test Kitchen: Holland House ®

CRISPY FISH FILLETS

1/4 cup frozen Minute Maid[R] Lemonade
    Concentrate, thawed and undiluted
1/4 cup butter or margarine, melted
1/2 teaspoon salt
1/8 teaspoon pepper
1/2 cup crushed onion-flavored crackers
2 pounds fresh red snapper, halibut or sole fillets

Combine lemonade concentrate, butter, salt and pepper; and 1/4 cup lemonade mixture to crushed crackers. Mix well. Place fillets in square baking pan. Pour remaining lemonade mixture over fillets; sprinkle with cracker mixture. Bake at 400⁰ for 25 to 30 minutes until fish flakes.

Makes 4 to 6 servings

Test Kitchen: Minute Maid ®

TERIYAKI FISH ROLLS

6 slices day-old bread, cut into 1/2-inch cubes
1/2 cup finely chopped celery
1/2 cup finely chopped onion
1/2 cup butter or margarine, melted
12 fresh or frozen fish fillets; thawed, if frozen
1/2 cup Kikkoman Teriyaki Sauce

Combine bread cubes, celery, onion and butter; set aside. Brush fillets with portion of teriyaki sauce, making sure each piece is well coated. Divide stuffing into 12 equal portions; spread on each fillet. Roll fillets up jell-roll fashion and place in shallow baking pan, seam side down. Brush fish rolls thoroughly with remaining teriyaki sauce. Bake in 350ºF oven 30 minutes, or until fish flakes easily when tested with fork, basting frequently.

Makes 6 servings

Test Kitchen: Kikkoman International Inc. ®

CIOPPINO--San Francisco Fish Stew

2 cans (8 ounce) Bumble Bee Whole Oysters
12 clams, washed
2 1/2 cups water
3 cups sliced Dole Fresh Mushrooms
2 cloves garlic, minced
1 large onion, chopped
1/4 cup olive oil
6 large tomatoes, seeded and chopped
1 can (6 ounces) tomato paste
1 cup red wine
2 teaspoons sugar
1 teaspoon oregano, crumbled
1 teaspoon salt
1 pound (1-inch thick) rock cod fish
1/4 pound cooked baby shrimp
Chopped parsley for garnish

Drain oysters, reserving liquid. Stem clams in water 3 minutes until they open. Reserve water. In a heavy kettle, saute mushrooms, garlic, paper and onion in oil until onion is soft. Stir in reserved oyster liquid, reserved water, tomatoes, tomato paste, wine, sugar, oregano and salt. Cover, simmer 30 minutes. Cut rock cod into bite-size chunks. Add to kettle with shrimp, clams and oysters. Cook 3 to 5 minutes until fish is just tender. Remove from heat. Garnish with parsley.

Makes 3 quarts

Test Kitchen: Castle & Cooke/Bumble Bee ®

ALMOND SALMON TURNOVERS

Pastry for double crust pie
2 tablespoons butter or margarine
1 cup sliced fresh mushrooms
1/2 cup chopped onion
1/2 cup chopped green pepper
1 tablespoon flour
1/4 teaspoon marjoram, crushed
1/4 teaspoon thyme, crushed
1/4 teaspoon salt
1/3 cup milk
1 can (16 ounce) salmon, drained and flaked
1 cup Blue Diamond^R Blanched Slivered Almonds,
   toasted
4 ounces Mozzarella cheese, grated

Prepare pastry according to favorite recipe or package directions. Divide pastry in half; cut each half into thirds. Roll each piece on a lightly floured surface into a 7-inch circle. Set aside. In medium saucepan, melt butter. Add mushrooms, onion and green pepper, cook until tender. Stir in flour, marjoram, thyme and salt. Cook over low heat, stirring, 3 to 4 minutes, or until bubbly. Stir in milk. Cook, stirring constantly over medium heat, until mixture just comes to a boil. Remove from heat. Stir in salmon and 3/4 cup of the almonds. Spoon salmon mixture onto half of each of the circles, leaving a 1/2-inch pastry border around the edges. Dampen edges of pastry with water. Fold top half of pastry over fillings; seal edges. Transfer with wide spatula to greased baking sheet. Cut a small slit in each turnover. Bake at 400°F, 15 minutes. Sprinkle with cheese and top with remaining almonds. Bake 5 minutes longer.

Note: 2 cans (7 ounces each) tuna may be substituted for the salmon.

Makes 6 servings

**Test Kitchen: California Almond Growers
                 Exchange**

SALMON QUICHE

1 10-inch unbaked pie shell
1 can (15 1/2 ounce) Bumble Bee Pink Salmon
1 package (9 ounce) frozen chopped spinach
1 1/2 cups shredded Monterey Jack cheese
1 package (3 ounce) cream cheese, softened
1/2 teaspoon salt
1/2 teaspoon thyme
4 eggs, lightly beaten
1 cup milk

Preheat oven to 375°F. Bake pie shell 10 minutes until partially set. Drain salmon. Mash bones. Cook spinach according to package directions. Drain well. Combine spinach, Monterey Jack cheese, cream cheese, salt and thyme. Arrange salmon and mashed bones into pie shell. Spoon spinach mixture on top. Combine eggs and milk. Pour over salmon and spinach. Bake in preheated oven 40 to 45 minutes. Let stand 10 minutes before serving.

Makes 6 to 8 servings

Test Kitchen: Castle & Cooke/Bumble Bee ®

SALMON SUPREME CREPES

1 (10 ounce) package Green Giant Tiny Peas
    with pea pods and water chestnuts frozen
    in Oriental butter sauce
2 (2 1/2 ounce) or 1 (4 1/2 ounce) jar whole
    mushrooms, drained
1/2 cup sliced green onions
1/3 cup butter or margarine
5 tablespoons flour
2 cups half and half cream
1/4 cup shredded Swiss cheese
1 teaspoon lemon juice
3/4 teaspoon salt
Dash cayenne
1 (15 3/4 ounce) can red salmon, drained and
    Makes 8 servings
Test Kitchen: Oscar Mayer
 flaked
16 crepes
1/2 cup shredded Swiss cheese
Grated Parmesan cheese

Cook Green Giant Peas according to package
directions. While peas are cooking, saute mushrooms
and green onions in butter until onions are translucent.
Stir in flour until creamy. Add cream in gradual
amounts, stirring after each addition to prevent lumps.
Heat, stirring constantly, until thickened and smooth.
Add cheese, lemon juice, salt, cayenne, salmon and

continued on next page...

peas; heat and stir until cheese is melted. Fill 16 crepes with creamed salmon mixture and fold over. Place in 2 shallow baking dishes. Spoon remaining creamed salmon, if any, down the centers of the folded crepes. Sprinkle the 1/2 cup shredded Swiss cheese down the centers and sprinkle generously with Parmesan cheese. Bake in preheated 350ºF degree oven for 25 to 30 minutes or until heated through and cheese is melted.

Makes 8 servings

Test Kitchen: Green Giant Company ®

SESAME SALMON BOATS

1 can (7 3/4 ounce) Bumble Bee Red Salmon
1 avocado
Crisp salad greens
Lemon juice
1/4 cup mayonnaise
1/4 teaspoon dill weed
1/4 teaspoon garlic salt
2 teaspoons toasted sesame seeds

Drain salmon. Remove skin, if desired. Mash bones. Halve avocado; remove seed. Place each half on a salad plate lined with crisp salad greens. Sprinkle with lemon juice. Combine mayonnaise, dill weed, garlic salt and 1 teaspoon sesame seeds. Fold in salmon and mashed bones. Spoon into avocado halves. Sprinkle with remaining sesame seeds to serve.

Makes 2 servings
Test Kitchen: Castle & Cooke/Bumble Bee ®

TUESDAYS SPECIAL

1 can (15 1/2 ounce) Bumble Bee Pink Salmon
3 cups egg noodles
5 cups boiling water
2 cups sliced Dole Fresh Mushrooms
1/4 cup butter
3 medium zucchini, sliced
2 cups sliced carrots
2 tablespoons flour
1 teaspoon dill weed
1 teaspoon salt
Dash nutmeg
1 3/4 cups milk
2 tablespoons sherry
1/2 cup grated Parmesan cheese

Drain salmon. Remove skin, if desired. Mash
bones. Cook noodles in boiling water 6 to 7 minutes.
Drain. Saute mushrooms in 2 tablespoons butter.
Remove mushrooms and combine with salmon, mashed
bones, noodles, zucchini and carrots. Melt remaining
butter in same skillet. Stir in flour, dill, salt and nutmeg
until blended. Gradually stir in milk, stirring constantly, until mixture boils and thickens. Remove from
heat. Stir in sherry. Stir into salmon and vegetable
mixture. Pour into 2-quart shallow casserole. Sprinkle
with Parmesan cheese. Bake in 350ºF oven 25 to 30
minutes.

Makes 4 to 6 servings
Test Kitchen: Castle & Cooke/Bumble Bee ®

WESTERN SALMON LOAF

1 can (15 1/2 ounce) Bumble Bee Pink Salmon
1 egg, lightly beaten
1 1/2 cups shredded Monterey Jack cheese
3 tablespoons wheat germ
1 cup cooked green noodles
1 cup cooked chopped broccoli
1/4 cup dairy sour cream
3/4 teaspoon oregano, crumbled
1 medium onion, diced
1 clove garlic, minced
1/2 cup diced celery
1 tablespoon oil
1 can (15 ounce) tomato sauce

Drain salmon. Remove skin, if desired. Mash bones. Combine salmon and bones with egg, 1 cup cheese and wheat germ. Combine noodles, broccoli, sour cream, remaining 1/2 cup cheese and 1/4 teaspoon oregano. Saute onion, garlic and celery in oil until onion is soft. Stir in tomato sauce and remaining 1/2 teaspoon oregano. Simmer 15 minutes. Combine one-half with salmon mixture. Spoon one-half salmon mixture in well-greased square 1-quart casserole dish. Soon broccoli mixture on top. Top with remaining salmon mixture. Bake in a 375°F oven 35 to 40 minutes. Let stand 10 minutes before serving. Warm remaining tomato sauce mixture and spoon over each serving.

Makes 4 servings
Test Kitchen: Castle & Cooke/Bumble Bee ®

SEAFOOD KABOBS IN PLUM SAUCE

1 can (3 3/4 ounce) Bumble Bee Smoked Oysters
1/4 pound cooked baby shrimp
1 green pepper, cut in chunks
8 to 10 cherry tomatoes
8 to 10 water chestnuts
3 tablespoons butter
1/3 cup plum jam
1 tablespoon white wine vinegar
1/4 teaspoon onion powder

Drain oysters. Arrange oysters alternately with shrimp, green pepper chunks, cherry tomatoes and water chestnuts on 6-inch skewers. Melt butter over low heat. Add plum jam, stirring until melted. Stir in white wine vinegar and onion powder. Place kebabs on rack in broiler pan. Brush with sauce. Broil 5 inches from heat, turning and basting 3 to 5 minutes.

Makes 6 to 8 skewers

Test Kitchen: Castle & Cooke/Bumble Bee ®

SHRIMP JAMBALAYA

4 slices bacon
1/2 cup chopped onion
1/2 cup chopped green pepper
1/2 cup uncooked long grain rice
1 1/2 cups Minute Maid^R Orange Juice,
  reconstituted
1 teaspoon salt
1 tablespoon Worcestershire sauce
1 can (1 pound) tomatoes, undrained
1 can (8 ounce) tomato sauce
2 cloves garlic, minced
2 cups frozen shrimp
1 package (10 ounce) frozen okra, partially
  thawed and sliced
1/4 cup sherry, if desired

In large fry pan, or Dutch oven, fry bacon until crisp; remove bacon and crumble. In bacon drippings, saute onion and green pepper until tender crisp. Add remaining ingredients except shrimp, okra, sherry and crumbled bacon; cover and simmer for 30 minutes until rice is tender. Add remaining ingredients. Simmer, uncovered, for about 15 minutes until okra is tender.

Makes 6 to 8 servings.

Test Kitchen: Minute Maid ®

SEAFOOD QUICHE

10 ounces crabmeat, or fresh shrimp (deveined)
   or fish fillet (cubed)
1 tablespoon chopped celery
1 tablespoon chopped onion
1 tablespoon finely chopped parsley
2 tablespoons cooking sherry
4 eggs, lightly beaten
2 cups cream or 2 cups each milk and cream
1/4 teaspoon nutmeg
1 1/2 tablespoons Old Bay Seasoning

Combine first five ingredients in mixing bowl. Refrigerate one half hour. Preheat over to 450°F. Prepare a 9-inch 1-crust pie recipe. Line a 9-inch pie plate with pastry. Bake five minutes. Sprinkle the inside of the partly baked pastry shell with seafood mixture. Combine eggs, cream, nutmeg, Old Bay Seasoning and pour over seafood mixture in the pie shell. Bake 15 minutes at 450°F, reduce oven temperature to 350°F and bake until a knife inserted one inch from the pastry edge comes out clean. Serve immediately. Can also be served as an hors doeuvre.

Makes 6 to 8 servings.

Test Kitchen: The Baltimore Spice Company ®

CARIBBEAN BUTTERFLY SHRIMP

1 pound large shrimp
1 tablespoon butter
1 tablespoon oil
2/3 cup chopped onion
2/3 cup chopped celery
3/4 teaspoon dill weed
2 cups sliced green Dole Bananas
1 teaspoon paprika
1 cup dry white wine
1 cup water
4 chicken bouillon cubes, crumbled
1 tablespoon cornstarch
2 tablespoons chopped parsley
2 teaspoons lemon juice
Hot cooked rice

Shell and butterfly shrimp, removing vein. Heat butter and oil in 10-inch skillet. Add onion, celery and dill and saute until tender, about 3 minutes. Add shrimp and bananas, and saute 5 minutes. Stir in paprika. Combine wine, water, bouillon cubes and cornstarch and add to skillet. cook, stirring gently, until mixture boils and thickens. Stir in parsley and lemon juice. Serve at once over hot cooked rice.

Make 4 servings.

Test Kitchen: Castle & Cooke/Dole ®

SHRIMP CREOLE

2 tablespoons butter or margarine
3/4 cup chopped onion
1/2 cup chopped green pepper
1/4 cup chopped celery
1 (6 ounce) can tomato paste
2 cups water
2 to 3 teaspoons Old Bay Seasoning, depending
    on heat preference
1 teaspoon salt
1 bay leaf, whole or crushed
2 cups cleaned cooked shrimp
3 cups hot cooked rice or spaghetti

In 10-inch skillet saute onion and green pepper in butter until tender. Stir in remaining ingredients except shrimp and rice or spaghetti. Cook over low heat stirring occasionally, about 20 minutes. Stir in shrimp, heat through about 10 minutes. Serve over rice or spaghetti.

Makes 6 servings

Test Kitchen: The Baltimore Spice Company ®

PACIFIC COAST CREPES

2 eggs
2/3 cup milk
1/2 cup flour
1 tablespoon butter melted
1/2 teaspoon salt
Oil

Beat together eggs, milk, flour, melted butter and salt until smooth. Cover and chill several hours. Heat a 7-inch skillet or crepe pan over low heat. Brush with oil; pour in 2 to 3 tablespoons batter, tilting pan to spread batter evenly. Cook until browned; turn and brown other side. Repeat with remaining batter, making 8 crepes in all.

FILLING:
1/4 cup butter
2 cups sliced Dole Fresh Mushrooms
1/2 cup sliced green onion
2 tablespoons flour
1/2 teaspoon salt
1/2 teaspoon fines herbes
1/2 cup half & half
1/3 cup dry white wine
1/2 pound fresh cooked bay shrimp
Dairy sour cream

Melt 2 tablespoons butter in a large skillet. Saute mushrooms and green onion until just tender; remove

continued on next page...

from pan. Add remaining 2 tablespoons butter. Blend in flour, salt and fines herbes. Gradually add half & half, stirring constantly. Stir in wine. Cook to medium thickness. Fold in shrimp and sauted vegetables. Fill each crepe with about 2 tablespoons filling; roll and place on a heat-proof platter. Cover loosely with foil. Heat in a 300°F oven 15 to 20 minutes. Serve topped with sour cream.

Makes 4 servings

Test Kitchen: Castle & Cooke/Dole ®

FILLETS OF SOLE CARTAGENA

1/3 cup unblanched almonds
3 tablespoons grated Parmesan cheese
1/2 teaspoon salt
1/4 teaspoon dill weed
1/4 teaspoon paprika
1 pound sole fillets
1 tablespoon butter
1 tablespoon oil
2 medium Dole Bananas
1 tablespoon lemon juice

Turn almonds into blender and blend fine (or grate, using Mouli grater). Mix with cheese, salt, dill and paprika on sheet of waxed paper. Dip fillets one at a time in the mixture, coating both sides. Heat butter and oil in 10-inch skillet. Add sole in single layer and brown over moderate heat, turning once, and cooking each fillet about 5 minutes, just until fish is browned and flakes easily. Remove to heated serving platter. Peel bananas and halve crosswise. Add to skillet, along with lemon juice. Cook 1 minute, shaking skillet to turn bananas, so they cook on all sides. Arrange on serving platter with fish, and serve at once.

Makes 4 servings

Test Kitchen: Castle & Cooke/Dole ®

FILLET OF SOLE VERONIQUE

Butter
2 tablespoons green onions, chopped
8 sole filets
White pepper
3/4 cup Holland House White Cooking Wine
Water
2 tablespoons flour
1 cup milk
1 egg yolk slightly beaten
1 cup seedless white grapes (canned or fresh)
2 tablespoons whipped cream

Coat the bottom of a saucepan with butter, add chopped green onions and sole filets that have been rolled and secured with toothpicks. Sprinkle filets with a little white pepper and add 3/4 cup white wine and 1/2 cup water. Cover the top of the pan with butchers paper in which you have punched a hole in the center about the size of a dime. Place pan over medium heat and when it reaches the boiling point , cover, simmer gently for 8 to 10 minutes or until filets are fork tender. Remove filets to warm heat-proof platter and discard toothpicks. Reduce liquid in which fish was cooked until about 1/2 cup remains. In another saucepan melt 2 tablespoons of butter, blend in 2 tablespoons flour, remove pan from heat and very gradually add 1 cup milk, blending it in carefully until sauce is smooth. Return to heat and cook slowly stirring constantly until sauce begins to thicken. Add a few tablespoons of the hot sauce to a dish containing

continued on next page

a lightly beaten egg yolk and mix well. Add egg mixture to saucepan and stir until sauce is smooth and thick. Add this cream sauce to mixture in which fish was cooked and fold 2 tablespoons whipped cream into sauce and pour it over fish on platter. Place white grapes around fish (if grapes are fresh, simmer in water for a few minutes) and put platter under the broiler flame for several minutes until top is browned.

Makes 4 servings

Test Kitchen: Holland House ®

continued on next page

STUFFED TROUT

1/2 cup celery, chopped
1/2 cup green onions, chopped, including tops
1 garlic clove, minced
8 tablespoons butter or margarine
1 cup stale bread crumbs
1/2 pound broiled shrimp, chopped
1/2 pound lump crab meat
2 tablespoons chopped parsley
1 egg, slightly beaten
Dash cayenne pepper
1/4 cup Holland House Marsala Cooking Wine
Salt, freshly ground pepper to taste
4 trout, medium size
4 tablespoons lemon juice
3 tablespoons melted butter or margarine

In a skillet, saute celery, onion and garlic in melted butter over low heat. Add bread crumbs, shrimp, crab meat, parsley, egg, cayenne and Marsala; mix well. Season to taste with salt and freshly ground pepper. Remove from heat. Split thick side of trout, lengthwise and crosswise; loosen meat from bone of fish to form a pocket for stuffing. Brush well with melted butter and lemon juice; salt and pepper if desired, and stuff pocket. Place in pan with enough water to cover bottom. Broil 3 inches from heat until fish flakes easily with fork. Baste every few minutes with liquid in the pan. If desired, trout may also be placed in a large skillet and cooked in a preheated 400°F oven for about 20 minutes until done, basting every few minutes with the lemon juice and butter.

Makes 4 servings
Test Kitchen: Holland House ®

STUFFED TROUT COCO ALMONDINE

4 small trout, 3/4 pound each
1/2 cup Coco Casa Cream of Coconut
2 tablespoons olive oil
4 tablespoons lemon juice
4 tablespoons sliced almonds, lightly toasted
4 boiled shrimp for garnish (optional)

Rinse trout and pat dry. Sprinkle with salt and brush thoroughly with cream of coconut and olive oil. Sprinkle with lemon juice. Fill cavity with stuffing and place fish side by side in ovenproof dish. Slide any leftover stuffing under fish. Broil at 450°F on middle shelf of oven for 10 minutes, basting occasionally with cream of coconut. Turn fish over, baste again, and cook ten minutes more. Sprinkle with almonds.

Stuffing for trout:
2 carrots
2 stalks celery
1 small onion
3 sprigs parsley
3 tablespoons butter

1/4 pound shrimp, chopped
1/4 cup Coco Casa Cream of Coconut
4 tablespoons bread crumbs
2 tablespoons sliced almonds, toasted
2 tablespoons coconut flakes
1/2 teaspoon salt

Finely chop carrots, celery, onion and parsley.
Cook mixture gently in butter for 4 minutes. Remove
from heat and stir in remaining ingredients.

Makes 4 servings.

Test Kitchen: Coco Ribe ®

TUNA FRITTATA

1 can (9 1/4 ounce) Bumble Bee Chunk Light Tuna*
1/4 pound bacon, diced
1 small onion, chopped
1/2 pound zucchini, sliced
6 eggs
1/2 cup grated Parmesan cheese
1/2 teaspoon thyme, crumbled

Drain tuna. Fry bacon in 9-inch skillet over moderate heat until golden. Drain bacon on absorbent towels. Saute onion and zucchini in bacon drippings. Combine bacon, eggs, 1/4 cup cheese, thyme and tuna. Pour over zucchini mixture. Cover and cook over moderate heat 8 to 10 minutes until eggs are set but still moist on top. Sprinkle remaining 1/4 cup cheese over top. Place 4 inches under broiler and heat 3 minutes until cheese melts and is golden. Leftovers may be refrigerated and served cold.

*or use 2 cans (6 1/2 ounce each) Bumble Bee Chunk Light Tuna

Makes 6 servings

Test Kitchen: Castle & Cooke/Bumble Bee ®

STEAMED SESAME TUNA

1 can (12 1/2 ounce) Bumble Chunk LIght Tuna*
Water
1 teaspoon sesame seeds, toasted
1 stalk green onion, chopped
2 tablespoons soy sauce
2 tablespoons vegetable oil or sesame oil
Chinese parsley for garnish

Drain tuna. Turn tuna into a heat-proof shallow dish set over a rack in a skillet filled with about 1/2 inch of water. Cover and steam tuna about 5 minutes. Toss in sesame seeds, green onion and soy sauce. Heat oil and carefully pour over tuna. Garnish with parsley. Makes 4 servings.

*or use 2 cans (6 1/2 ounce each) Bumble Bee Chunk Light Tuna

Makes 4 servings

Test Kitchen: Castle & Cooke/Bumble Bee ®

SUPER SOUFFLE

1 can (9 1/4 ounce) Bumble Bee Chunk Light
  Tuna*
1/4 cup butter
1/3 cup flour
1 cup milk
5 eggs, separated
1/4 teaspoon pepper
3 tablespoons chopped green onion
1 cup shredded Cheddar cheese

Drain tuna. Melt butter over medium heat. Stir
in flour until blended. Gradually add milk, stirring
constantly. Remove from heat. Beat in egg yolks and
pepper. Stir in onions, cheese and tuna. Beat egg
whites until stiff; fold into cheese mixture. Turn into a
1 1/2 quart buttered souffle dish. Bake on middle shelf
in 375°F oven 45 minutes. Serve immediately.

*or use 1 can (6 1/2 ounce) Bumble Bee Chunk
Light Tuna

Makes 6 servings

Test Kitchen: Castle & Cooke/Bumble Bee ®

TUNA CURRY CASSEROLE

4 strips bacon, cut in 1-inch pieces
3 tablespoons butter
2 cups sliced Dole Fresh Mushrooms
3 tablespoons chopped green onion
1 tablespoon curry powder
1 can (14 1/2 ounce) whole tomatoes
2 cans (7 ounce) Bumble Bee Solid White
   Albacore Tuna
1 tablespoon lime juice
3 cups fluffy buttered rice
1/4 cup water

Fry bacon pieces until crisp; remove and drain. Pour off all but 1 tablespoon bacon fat. Add 2 tablespoons butter to skillet. Saute mushrooms and onion until just tender; remove from pan. Add remaining butter and curry to pan. Cook and stir about 1 minute. Add tomatoes with all liquid, breaking up tomatoes with a spoon. Simmer about 5 minutes. Drain tuna; add to curry sauce along with lime juice. Remove from heat. Combine fluffy rice with bacon and sauteed vegetables. Turn rice mixture into a 2-quart casserole dish. Spoon tuna-curry sauce over rice. Pour water over all. Cover and bake in a 350°F oven until bubbly and hot, about 20 minutes.

Makes 8 servings

Test Kitchen: Castle & Cooke/Bumble Bee ®

GAZAPACHO SEAFOOD FILLETS

3 tablespoons butter
1 small onion, diced
3 medium tomatoes, diced
1 cucumber, pared and diced
1 can (8 ounce) Dole Chunk Pineapple in Juice
1/4 teaspoon thyme, crumbled
1/4 teaspoon garlic powder
1 tablespoon sherry
2 turbot fish fillets (3 to 4 ounces each)

Melt butter in large, heavy skillet. Saute onion over medium-high heat until golden, about 5 minutes. Add diced tomatoes and cucumber and simmer uncovered about 10 minutes until sauce reduces and thickens. Reduce heat to low. Stir in undrained pineapple chunks and seasonings. Stir in sherry. Place fish fillets on top of sauce. Cover tightly and steam until fish is cooked., about 5 minutes (depending upon thickness of fish). Carefully remove cooked fish from skillet with slotted spoon. Serve with sauce.

Makes 2 servings

Test Kitchen: Castle & Cooke/Dole ®

NOTES

NOTES

NOTES

NOTES

NOTES